College Science Teachers
Guide to
Assessment

College Science Teachers

Guide to
Assessment

Editors
Thomas R. Lord
Donald P. French
Linda W. Crow

National Science Teachers Association

Arlington, Virginia

National Science Teachers Association

Claire Reinburg, Director
Jennifer Horak, Managing Editor
Judy Cusick, Senior Editor
Andrew Cocke, Associate Editor
Betty Smith, Associate Editor

ART AND DESIGN
Will Thomas, Jr., Director
Joseph Butera, Graphic Designer, cover and interior design

PRINTING AND PRODUCTION
Catherine Lorrain, Director
Nguyet Tran, Assistant Production Manager
Jack Parker, Electronic Prepress Technician

NATIONAL SCIENCE TEACHERS ASSOCIATION
Francis Q. Eberle, PhD, Executive Director
David Beacom, Publisher

LIBRARY OF CONGRESS CATALOGING-IN-PUBLICATION DATA

College science teachers guide to assessment / Thomas Lord, Donald French, and Linda Crow, editors.
     p. cm.
 Includes index.
 ISBN 978-1-933531-11-3
 1. Science—Study and teaching (Higher)—Methodology. 2. Science—Study and teaching (Higher)—Evaluation.
3. Academic achievement—Evaluation. 4. Educational tests and measurements. I. Lord, Thomas R. II. French,
Donald P., 1952- III. Crow, Linda W.
 Q181.C535 2009
 507.1'1—dc22
                          2008041750

NSTA is committed to publishing material that promotes the best in inquiry-based science education. However, conditions of actual use may vary, and the safety procedures and practices described in this book are intended to serve only as a guide. Additional precautionary measures may be required. NSTA and the authors do not warrant or represent that the procedures and practices in this book meet any safety code or standard of federal, state, or local regulations. NSTA and the authors disclaim any liability for personal injury or damage to property arising out of or relating to the use of this book, including any of the recommendations, instructions, or materials contained therein.

Table of Contents

Table of Contents

Section 3. How-To Section
Successful Classroom-Tested Practices and
Instructions and Rubrics for Their Implementation

Table of Contents

Section 4. General Practices to Improve Assessment

Contributors

Brown, Mary H.
Lansing Community College
MC 5400–Science
411 N. Grand Ave.
Lansing, MI 48901
Brownm@lcc.edu

Cheesman, Kerry L.
Capital University
Columbus, OH
kcheesma@capital.edu

Coleman, Anne
Department of Life and Physical Sciences
Cabrini College
610 King of Prussia Rd.
Radnor, PA 19087
annecoleman@cabrini.edu

Cohen, Robert A.
Department of Physics
East Stroudsburg University
East Stroudsburg, Pennsylvania
rcohen@po-box.esu.edu

Cudaback, Cynthia
Marine Earth and Atmospheric Science
Campus Box 8208
North Carolina State University
cynthia_cudaback@ncsu.edu

Dean, Karol
Mount St. Mary's College
12001 Chalon Rd.
Los Angeles, CA 90049
kdean@msmc.la.edu

Eason, Grace
University of Maine at Farmington
173 High St., Preble Hall
Farmington, ME 04938
geason@maine.edu

Gallo, Mark A.
Niagara University
DePaul Hall,
Niagara University, NY 14109
mgallo@niagara.edu

Gomez-Zwiep, Susan
California State University, Long Beach
Department of Science Education
Long Beach, CA 90840
sgomezwp@csulb.edu

Haviland, Don
California State University, Long Beach
1250 Bellflower Blvd.
Long Beach, CA 90808-2201
dhavilan@csulb.edu

Kandlbinder, Peter
Institute for Interactive Media and Learning,
University of Technology, Sydney
Peter.Kandlbinder@uts.edu.au

Lord, Thomas R.
Department of Biology
Indiana University of Pennsylvania
Indiana, PA 15705
trlord@iup.edu

Melvin, Thomas J.
Biology Department
Indiana University of Pennsylvania
Indiana, Pennsylvania 15705
t.j.melvin@iup.edu

Metz, Anneke M.
Department of Cell Biology and Neuroscience
Montana State University
Bozeman, MT 59717
anneke@montana.edu

Contributors

Rybarczyk, Brian J.
The Graduate School
University of North Carolina/Chapel Hill
CB#4010
Chapel Hill, NC 27599-4010
brybar@unc.edu

Siebert, Eleanor D.
Mount St. Mary's College
12001 Chalon Rd.
Los Angeles, CA 90049
esiebert@msmc.la.edu

Sorensen, Kathryn H.
Biology Department
American River College
4700 College Oak Dr.
Sacramento, CA 95841
SorensKH@arc.losrios.edu

Straits, William J.
California State University, Long Beach
Department of Science Education
Long Beach, CA 90840
wstraits@csulb.edu

Swails, Nancy J.
Capital University
Columbus, OH 43209
swails@capital.edu

Tichenor, Linda
Department of Biology
University of Arkansas
Fort Smith, Arkansas 72913
lticheno@uafortsmith.edu

Travis, Holly
Department of Biology
Indiana University of Pennsylvania
Indiana, Pennsylvania 15705
holly.travis@iup.edu

von Bergmann, HsingChi
EDT 726, Faculty of Education
University of Calgary
Calgary, AB, Canada T2N 1N4
hsingchi@ucalgary.ca

Waldvogel, Jerry A.
Department of Biological Sciences
Clemson University
Clemson, SC 29634-0314
waldvoj@clemson.edu

Walton, Kristen
Department of Biology
Missouri Western State University
4525 Downs Dr.
St. Joseph, MO 64507
kwalton1@missouriwestern.edu

Wilke, R. Russell
Angelo State University
Department of Biology
ASU Station - 10890
San Angelo, TX 76909
russell.wilke@angelo.edu

Wood, Bonnie S.
University of Maine at Presque Isle
181 Main St.
Presque Isle, ME 04769
bonnie.s.wood@umpi.edu

Yerger, Ellen
Department of Biology
Indiana University of Pennsylvania
114 Weyandt Hall
Indiana, Pennsylvania 15701
ellen.yerger@iup.ed

Preface: Note From the Editors

Welcome to the sixth in the series of SCST monographs created by the members of the Executive Board of the Society for College Science Teachers in cooperation with the National Science Teachers Association. This document covers an extremely important and often controversial topic, that of evaluating the value of students and professorial works. The jointly sponsored monograph has been three years in the making with the initial agreement with the National Science Teachers Association taking place in the fall of 2006.

Each submission in this monograph was reviewed by at least two members on the Editorial Board with the published authors responding to reviewers critiques and providing the final proofing of their own entry. Articles were selected on the quality of the writing and their contribution to the value and importance of assessment in a college science setting.

The monograph examines assessment issues from several different viewpoints and is broken into several chapters. The first section deals with general assessment topics such as validation of survey instruments and creating a culture for faculty-owned assessment. The second section concerns traditional and alternative forms of assessment in both science and the science education classroom. The third section presents a series of how-to assessment practices that have been successfully utilized in the field. Finally, the fourth section provides a series of tips to enhance assessment in the college science classroom.

The editors would like to thank all the contributors to the monograph. The quality of the initiative is indicative of the time and energy they put into this work.

Thomas R. Lord
Indiana University of Pennsylvina
trlord@iup.edu

Donald P. French
Oklahoma State University
dfrench@okstate.edu

Linda W. Crow
Montgomery College
linda.w.crow@nhmccd.edu

Acknowledgments

The editors wish to thank Holly Travis for her tireless effort and dedication to the construction of this document. Thanks also to Ellen Yerger and Tom Melvin for their help in making this monograph a success.

SECTION 1

General Assessment Topics

Chapter 1

Survey Instrument Validation: The First Commandment of Educational Research

Cynthia Cudaback
Marine Earth and Atmospheric Science
North Carolina State University
Raleigh, North Carolina

And the Lord said unto them, "Thou shalt validate thy survey instrument," and they validated until it was good.

Survey instrument[1] validation may be the most difficult task for a scientist starting to conduct educational research. A survey that is perceived to be inadequately validated will generally be rejected for publication, but there is little guidance on how exactly to validate a survey instrument. This chapter is intended to provide an introduction to the process of survey instrument validation, for people whose expertise is in scientific research and teaching. The examples given are specific to my own interest in promoting ocean literacy (COSEE 2005) and stewardship through courses in introductory oceanography, but the principles apply to any educational research in the sciences.

Formal definitions of validity include four parts: *face validity, content validity, construct validity,* and *criterion-related validity* (CSU 1993). A survey has face validity if it looks clear and well organized; this is something a researcher determines before giving the survey to any students or colleagues. A survey has content validity if the questions fall into the area under study; in theory, experts in a given field will agree on what questions belong in that field. A survey with criterion-related validity is directly comparable to other measures of the same student attributes; for example, class grades

---

1 "Survey instrument" is just educational jargon for a survey.

should correlate with student responses to post-class surveys of content knowledge.

Construct validity—the requirement that the survey actually measures what it is intended to measure—is the most important requirement and the hardest to satisfy. The formal definition is that the theoretical concept matches the measuring device, and educational researchers have made the analogy that one cannot drive nails with a screwdriver. Neither statement really helps understand how one determines what students are actually thinking. A more helpful comment is that construct validation is an iterative process, analogous to building a log cabin and chinking the cracks as the wind and rain blow in (R. Beichner, personal communication).

The difficulty in establishing construct validity for even one survey question is illustrated by some potential responses to the question "Did dinosaurs ever coexist with humans?" If a scientist were to include such a question in a survey, with potential answers of yes and no, she or he would probably be thinking, "No, Dinosaurs went extinct 65 million years ago, during a mass extinction caused by an asteroid impact. Humans have only been around for about 5 million years." But one student might be thinking, "No, 'old' appearing dinosaur bones were buried by God, about 6,000 years ago, to test our faith in His revealed world. Dinosaurs never existed." This student would get the correct answer for reasons quite unrelated to science. Another student might think, "Yes, *Jurassic Park* was a documentary, right?" while yet another might think, "Yes, current paleontological research classifies birds as living, feathered dinosaurs." One student got an incorrect answer due to spurious reasoning, and one student actually has a better answer than the scientist's original one! (Thanks to J. Libarkin for this example.)

In my efforts to develop a valid survey instrument, by trial and error, I have found some key principles:

- Start with qualitative data and work toward quantitative data.
- Listen to your students.

- Look at the data several ways and watch for surprises.
- Listen to experts, but trust yourself.

It is best to start with qualitative data, such as open-ended written questions. There is no point in asking students whether they think *a*, *b*, or *c* if they actually think *d* and *e*. Libarkin and Kurdziel (2002a, b) advocate using qualitative data to establish the context for the study, analyzing the qualitative data using quantitative methods, and finally developing new surveys that produce quantitative data. For example, the open-ended question, "Where have you learned about the ocean, before this class?" produces qualitative data, but it is easy to count the number of students mentioning different sources of information. When I asked that question, most students mentioned formal education, about 25% mentioned conversations with friends and family, and almost none mentioned aquaria or museums (Cudaback 2006). In later surveys, I listed all categories mentioned by students and asked them to circle their main sources of information. This question is considered more quantitative and also produced qualitatively different results—the number of students choosing informal education increased dramatically. The number of students mentioning friends and family remained constant, but had I not started with an open-ended question, I would not have known to include that category. The process of working from qualitative to quantitative surveys is crucial.

Listening to students is the best way to learn what they are thinking. The standard method for this is the "think aloud" interview (e.g., Adams et al. 2006). Students fill out the survey while thinking out loud. These interviews are taped for further study and can reveal students' understanding of the questions. This process, however, is very time-consuming. One shudders to think how many interviews must be conducted to find the very rare student who knows that birds are now considered to be dinosaurs. Fortunately, written surveys can allow students to comment on their thinking. J. Lambert (2005) and others actually provide two parts to each question—the question itself and a space for students' reasoning. In my own surveys, I have often learned about students' thinking from marginal notes. In all cases, it is important to start with a low-tech survey format that allows comments. Never start with a rigid format such as fill-in-the-bubble forms or online surveys.

It has been said that scientific discovery is announced, not with "Eureka!" but with "That's strange." Similarly, surprising data can greatly aid survey instrument validation. For example, on an attitude survey, one student with otherwise expert attitudes about the relevance of ocean science to the real world agreed with the statement, "Knowledge in oceanography consists of many disconnected topics." He responded to my query with a thoughtful discussion of the interdisciplinary nature of the science, and I soon realized that many students were interpreting the question in that light. After discussing the question with my students, I reworded it to say, "Topics in oceanography are not related to each other."

I have also been surprised by student responses to content surveys. My survey instrument alludes to the surprising fact that the feces of one dog contain enough bacteria to close down a beach in California. Students are very impressed with this, but most answered the question incorrectly on a postclass survey. It turned out that they did not know the meaning of the word "negligible." Similarly, when most students answered a version of this question correctly on later preclass surveys, I learned that they were really thinking of multiple dogs instead of individual dogs. The multiple revisions of this question also remind us that it is insufficient to get student feedback on only the first version of a question or survey. The validation process is highly iterative.

Experts in your scientific field or in educational research can help validate your survey instrument, but you also need to trust yourself. I have asked dozens of scientists and educators simply to take my surveys, and most have been moved to comment on some aspect or another. Many

significant improvements have come from this. However, a question I consider very important is whether household plumbing is affected by the Coriolis force. Many of my colleagues consider this pervasive myth beneath their notice, but if students think plumbing is affected by the Earth's rotation, they really do not understand that the ocean is vastly bigger than their toilets.

For me, this is the most important point. The ocean is vastly larger than we are, but we have tremendous power to harm it. My personal mission is to encourage my colleagues to teach introductory oceanography courses in a way that promotes both scientific understanding and informed stewardship of the ocean. The survey instrument I have developed is intended to test the hypothesis that teaching science in the context of stewardship improves students understanding of the nature and relevance of science. I hope that my experiences developing the survey are of use to other scientists embarking on their own educational missions.

References

Adams, W. K., K. K. Perkins, N. S. Podelefsky, M. Dubson, D. Finkelstein, and C. E. Wieman. 2006. A new instrument for measuring student beliefs about physics and learning physics: The Colorado learning attitudes about science survey. *Physical Review Special Topics—Physics Education Research.* Available online at *http://prst-per.aps.org/pdf/PRSTPER/v2/i1/e010101.*

Centers for Ocean Sciences Education Excellence (COSEE). 2005. Ocean literacy: The essential principles of ocean sciences. Available online at *www.coexploration.org/oceanliteracy/documents/OceanLitChart.pdf.*

Colorado State University (CSU). 1993. Reliability and validity. Available online at *http://writing.colostate.edu/guides/research/relval/index.cfm.*

Cudaback, C. N. 2006. What do college students know about the ocean? *Eos* 87: 418.

Lambert, J. 2005. Students' conceptual understandings of science after participating in a high school marine science course. *Journal of Geoscience Education* 44:385–394.

Libarkin, J. C., and S. W. Anderson. 2005. Assessment of learning in entry-level geoscience courses: Results from the geoscience concept inventory. *Journal of Geoscience Education* 53 (4): 394–401. Available online at *http://newton.bhsu.edu/eps/gci.html*

Libarkin, J. C., and J. P. Kurdziel. 2002a: Strategies for productive assessment, *Journal of Geoscience Education* 49 (3): 300–304.

Libarkin, J. C., and J. P. Kurdziel. 2002b: Assessing students' alternative conceptions. *Journal of Geoscience Education* 49 (4): 378–383.

Chapter 2

Building a Culture of Faculty-Owned Assessment

Don Haviland
California State University, Long Beach
Long Beach, California

Karol Dean
Mount St. Mary's College
Los Angeles, California

Eleanor D. Siebert
Mount St. Mary's College
Los Angeles, California

Introduction

As college or university faculty, most of us recognize the value of assessing student learning in the courses we teach. What may not always be as clear is the importance of assessing learning outcomes at the programmatic and institutional level as opposed to classroom or course assessment. However, today, perhaps more than ever, our institutions need to know and demonstrate just how our programs contribute to student learning.

Assessment is a process or tool to support effective teaching and learning—not an end in itself. We have defined *assessment* as the systematic collection of data on student learning, based on clearly defined outcomes, to inform pedagogy, curricula, and administrative decisions. In this definition, programs articulate outcomes, collect data, and then *act* on their findings. It is through this last step that faculty and institutions realize the potential of assessment.

The interest in assessing student learning has both internal and external dimensions. Internally, assessment of student learning is an important tool to improve learning—and teaching. It provides an opportunity for departments and programs to set curricular priorities *and* establishes the basis for making strategic decisions to improve learning. With a limited pool of resources, assessment information assists both faculty and administrators in providing more effective support for student learning. Assessment informs what we do in practice and allows an institution to direct attention and resources to areas of greatest need.

At the same time, external entities (such as current and prospective students, accrediting agencies, government bodies) are interested in the quality of learning that our institution and programs afford students. This interest is sparked both by the cost of higher education, particularly in the private sector, and the pressure to compete in our global economy. In authorizing the Commission on the Future of Higher Education, the Secretary of Education said, "It is time to examine how we can get the most out of our national investment in higher education. We have a responsibility to make sure our higher education system continues to meet our nation's needs for an educated and competitive workforce in the 21st century" (Spellings 2005). While the commission's final recommendations did not mirror the No Child Left Behind Act for K–12 education as closely as once feared, its work has sparked discussion about what steps higher education can take to address external pressures while maintaining its autonomy.

With so much at stake for both students and institutions, it is imperative that colleges and universities support faculty and others in comprehensive assessment efforts and act on changes suggested by assessment data. If higher education is to maintain its autonomy and programmatic diversity, assessment must be owned and implemented by faculty—not driven or imposed by external entities. Achieving this goal is no small challenge. This paper examines how we at Mount St. Mary's College[1] have sought to develop a culture of faculty-owned assessment.

Foundations for a Culture of Assessment

Mount St. Mary's College is similar to other colleges in several ways. We recognize the value of assessing student learning and are eager to do so

---

1   Mount St. Mary's College is a Catholic, master's university with a liberal arts tradition located in Los Angeles, California.

to support teaching and learning. Yet we are also a small university of roughly 2,500 students with limited resources, including a faculty with heavy teaching commitments and restricted time.

We began our effort to build a campuswide assessment program with a year of planning prior to implementation. As we did, we first sought to identify some of the core challenges and obstacles we expected to face along the way. These included:

- Faculty time: As a teaching-intensive college, our faculty spends most of their time teaching, grading, advising, and working with students outside of the classroom. Moreover, many faculty are already deeply involved in governance activities. As a result, faculty members are often very busy and have limited time for new initiatives.

- Skepticism: We knew some faculty would be skeptical about the goals of assessment and how the information might be used. Experience elsewhere has shown that some professors point to assessment as a tool for limiting academic freedom, imposing administrative control, or evaluating individual professors. We also were aware that some faculty might simply view assessment as the latest higher education fad, something that would lose traction and become extinct.

- Varying involvement: We realized that, despite our best efforts, some faculty would not participate in assessment. Even among those professors ready to participate, we expected that there would be varied amounts of time given to assessment, both across academic departments and programs and among individuals.

- Isolation: Much of the work in higher education takes place in the silos of the disciplines. We were committed to breaking down these walls whenever possible, giving faculty a chance to collaborate, share ideas, and support one another in this new effort.

Clear Values

Having defined the challenges, we then sought to articulate, both for ourselves and the college community, the values and principles that would guide our assessment efforts. Such principles have been outlined by scholars and practitioners in higher education, such as the now-defunct American Association for Higher Education (AAHE), which articulated nine principles (Astin et al. 1996). Drawing on the work of AAHE and others, we adopted the following core principles to guide our assessment work:

- *Assessment is linked to educational values.* To have an integrated system of assessment means there should be a direct line from institutional goals and mission, to campus-level student learning outcomes, to department- and major-level learning goals for students.
- *Assessment is comprehensive, systemic (affecting the whole institution), and systematic (intentional, taking place in a clear cycle).* Effective assessment is based on an intentional plan that outlines clear learning outcomes, collects data, and disseminates and uses the findings. Assessment should occur at all levels of the institution to recognize the multidimensional, holistic nature of student learning.
- *Assessment is a formative activity focused not on evaluating faculty or programs, but on supporting student learning and success.* While participation in assessment may be part of the program review or faculty review process, assessment *findings* must be seen as supporting a process of improvement rather than as a way for holding faculty and departments accountable.
- *Assessment findings must be put into practice.* An effective assessment system applies a model where findings from assessment are carefully reviewed and actions to improve the student learning experience are taken.
- *Assessment uses, whenever possible, multiple measures to document student learning outcomes.* This process of triangulation provides more reliable findings and recognizes the multidimen-

sional nature of student learning. However, this value must be balanced with what is feasible given available resources.

- *Assessment is the work of students, staff, and administrators.* Efforts should be led by the faculty, but they will require collaboration and involvement from all stakeholders and active support from institutional leaders.
- *Assessment is transparent.* All community members—staff, in addition to faculty—should be aware of the desired learning outcomes, data on those outcomes, and plans for change to support student learning.
- *Assessment succeeds when institutions use resources to provide technical and administrative support for the system.* Like most new initiatives, assessment takes resources. This may include support for faculty development in writing and measuring outcomes, administering reliable surveys, reassigning or buying-out faculty time, and other infrastructure elements required for an assessment system.

Having anticipated challenges and articulated values, we turned our efforts to more operational matters to develop and maintain momentum for engaging faculty with assessment.

The Main Steps

To implement a faculty-owned assessment program, we took several key steps. First, we researched what others have done with assessment and planned how we would move forward. Second, we held early and ongoing discussions of assessment in the college community. Third, we developed a structured way for faculty to spend time and receive support for their efforts in departmental assessment. Finally, college leaders gave visible and vocal support to assessment.

Planning

Since there had been little prior sustained work in assessment at the college, we wanted a clear plan for moving ahead with assessment, something that served as a visible roadmap to set goals and celebrate successes. We knew that our desire to move quickly necessitated the creation of a small, nimble group to develop and guide the plan. Ultimately, the Assessment Task Force, which was charged with developing that plan, consisted of three faculty members (one of whom chaired the task force), the director of assessment, and the academic deans of the two primary undergraduate programs on campus.[2]

The task force spent a year researching successful assessment efforts, developing a model for implementation, and securing funding to move forward. Task force members attended conferences on assessment, read about established practices, and researched successful programs to build their own expertise.[3]

It became clear that assessing curricular (e.g., general studies, graduate and undergraduate) and cocurricular programs would require different strategies. It could not be a "one size fits all" approach. We therefore decided to begin assessment work at the baccalaureate program level to maximize faculty interest and investment by helping faculty learn to do assessment where it mattered most to them. We believed that once faculty and other members of the college community were familiar with the process of assessment, it would be easier for them to apply the key principles to the general studies program, the graduate program, and to cocurricular programs.

---

2   Faculty who were also department chairs were solicited for participation because of their knowledge of the overall programs in their departments. A student affairs representative joined the group in its second year.

---

3   Because of limited resources for conferences, we found books, articles, and websites to be invaluable in building our expertise. One benefit of beginning work on assessment at this time is that there are multiple resources available for guidance, and a variety of models of how assessment can be done.

Communication

We recognized two-way communication as essential to building trust and creating a sustainable assessment program. Our goal was to talk about the "how" and "why" of assessment to educate our colleagues *and* to receive feedback from our colleagues on how to best meet their needs.

Once a multiyear plan had been developed during the first year of planning, members of the task force began making presentations about the plan to various campus constituencies (such as relevant faculty governance committees, department chairs, the faculty assembly, and the board of trustees). In these presentations, we stressed the centrality of faculty to assessment. We emphasized that, although the impetus to work on assessment came from accreditation expectations and college administrators, the form and shape of assessment would be created and sustained by faculty.

By discussing the upcoming implementation of assessment in multiple contexts during the first year, the community began to prepare for the work, and the task force was able to surface and address concerns well before the faculty were asked to participate in assessment. In addition, administrators learned that although assessment could be accomplished at relatively low cost, financial resources would be required to support faculty.

A Structure That Reflected Our Values

One element of the sustainable assessment system we envisioned was a structure that supported faculty effort by recognizing the time commitment involved and supporting professional development in the area.

Since time and energy are precious resources for faculty, we wanted to take some daily responsibilities away so that faculty could focus on assessment. Grant funds were used to give participants course release, and faculty appreciated this approach. This funding signaled the value given by the institution to assessment and the importance of faculty work in this area.

We adapted a model that had been successful in other college faculty development efforts by establishing Faculty Learning Communities (FLCs) of 7–8 faculty members each. One faculty member from each department served as the departmental representative and each FLC was facilitated by the director of assessment or the chair of the Assessment Task Force. These groups had two main goals: 1) to build FLC faculty skills in assessment so they could lead work in their departments; and, 2) to give FLC faculty structured time to talk about teaching and learning in relation to assessment.

The FLCs were roughly clustered by discipline, with the idea that teachers in related disciplines (e.g., sciences) might benefit from the ideas of their colleagues in developing student learning outcomes.[4] The groups met weekly for an hour over the academic year during the second year of our work. This structure allowed for the development of ideas over time, as faculty consulted with their departmental colleagues. In addition, the FLCs provided ongoing collegial support for faculty as they developed and revised their department assessment plans. They also allowed faculty to give feedback on the evolving assessment system.

While there are many steps to developing an assessment system (e.g., articulating outcomes, developing curricular maps), the FLCs had two broad tasks. First, in the fall semester, FLC participants were expected to lead their departments in establishing the framework of an assessment plan. This involved an iterative process in which department faculty worked together to identify learning outcomes, map these outcomes to the curriculum, and identify the evidence and criteria through which outcomes would be assessed.

Second, in the spring semester, FLC participants were expected to collaborate with their colleagues to finalize their multiyear assessment plans. In addition, they were tasked with leading the collection and analysis of data on two or

three of their learning outcomes. Faculty met to discuss results and draft action plans based on the findings. In many cases, the actions coming from these discussions had few if any financial implications. For example, faculty agreed to adjust their teaching practices, alter course sequences, or even change the rubric used in the assessment. For most departments, this process was the first time that student learning outcome data were systematically collected, analyzed, and acted upon by the full departmental faculty—and the faculty found the experience worthwhile.

To accomplish these tasks, the FLCs were given resources. An assessment handbook was compiled to provide guidance to faculty beginning this venture. As part of the handbook, templates were developed for the curriculum map, the overall assessment plan, and the data analysis retreat results. These templates allowed faculty to focus on the content, not the format; enhanced the ability to compare maps and plans across departments; and added consistency from an institutional perspective.

A second resource was guidance from experts, who were invited to talk with faculty about assessment. A nationally known assessment author and speaker visited the campus early in the academic year to conduct a daylong workshop on assessment basics that almost all faculty attended. Later in the year, a professor from the education department held a half-day workshop on rubric development, which was emerging as a key need for many departments.

Visible and Vocal Leadership

Whatever the external reasons to pursue assessment (e.g., accreditation), top college leaders viewed assessment, fundamentally, as a process for improving teaching, learning, and student success. Therefore, they undertook a sustained effort to communicate that belief to the campus community, reinforcing the idea that assessment activities were highly valued and worthwhile.

First, the college created the new position of director of assessment and institutional effectiveness.

4 An alternative organization, though, might have been to group departments by size (i.e., number of majors) as the final assessment plans might be similar.

The dedication of administrative resources to assessment sent a clear message about its importance to the institution. Second, in formal and informal talks to campus constituencies, the provost and the president continually emphasized the importance of assessment. For example, the provost declared "the year of assessment" at the opening faculty convocation as we began implementation.

Other support was even more tangible. The president used discretionary funds to support assessment-related department retreats. Finally, members of the Assessment Task Force were given time on the agendas of important faculty governance committees and at gatherings of the faculty to describe the current assessment efforts and to seek guidance and support for the next efforts. This leadership enhanced the ability to make large-scale progress in creating a culture of assessment.

The Results

More than two years into our effort, we have been pleased by the support and involvement of faculty and the progress made. While there is more to do, we now have a sound foundation for moving forward in developing a campuswide culture of assessment.

First, in spring 2007, the faculty adopted undergraduate learning outcomes for the college. These outcomes are based on the college mission and values. They provide a framework for organizing the goals of our general studies curriculum and serve as a base to which departments can align their outcomes. The collaborative, consultative process through which these outcomes were developed produced rich and productive discussions among faculty about educational values and curricula. The publication of these outcomes in the college catalog and other campus documents is a form of a promise to the community about the goals of the general studies curriculum and a Mount St. Mary's education.

Second, 13 of the 15 academic departments participating in the FLCs now have full, multi-year assessment plans related to their baccalaureate programs. Moreover, most of these programs have begun collecting and acting upon data on student learning. The assessment plans have been reviewed by the Assessment Task Force and feedback, based on a rubric, has been provided to programs to help them refine their plans.

Third, the college has a clear plan for moving forward with, and sustaining, assessment in the future. This includes funding for a designated faculty member in each department to continue facilitating assessment and an annual reporting structure to document findings and actions regarding assessment. The college is moving forward with integrating assessment into its other programs (associate and graduate) and will begin the challenge of assessing its general studies curriculum.

Fourth, there is a sense of momentum and buy-in for the process of assessment. While wariness has not been eliminated, many faculty seem to recognize the value of assessment. Having had the opportunity to collect, review, and act on outcomes data, faculty in many departments recognize that assessment can support their goal of effective teaching and learning. There is also a growing sense of trust as they realize the process is intended to be supportive rather than punitive.

Even with such progress, challenges and "to dos" remain. First, we recognize the need for more extensive faculty development on topics related to assessment. We would like to be able to send more faculty to assessment-related conferences (especially within their disciplines) so that they can become part of the wider national conversation and see firsthand what others are doing. In addition, we have identified needs for skill-specific workshops on topics such as developing and using rubrics, compiling and analyzing data, and even adjusting pedagogy in light of assessment findings.

Second, despite wide participation, not all faculty are involved directly in assessment. As a college with several small departments, we worry that individual faculty members who are trying to lead the assessment effort in their programs may be isolated and carry the burden—rather than acting as a facilitator of a collaborative effort. We continue to explore ways to get more faculty (including part-time faculty) involved and expand participation across departments.

Finally, we recognize the need to link assessment to decision-making structures. While not all assessment findings will have budget implications, some may. Institutional leaders must begin to expect departmental requests to be supported by assessment data and student learning goals when appropriate. Faculty buy-in and participation are more likely to grow when they see the process not only as worthwhile—but valued and rewarded by the institution.

Conclusion

Now more than two years into the process of developing an assessment system, we are certain of two things about assessment: (1) it takes work; and (2) it can be immensely worthwhile. However, the potential value of assessment can only be realized if findings are put into action. Unless student-learning data at the program and institutional level are systematically collected and acted upon, assessment will remain a reform with unrealized promise.

This emphasis on action is what makes faculty-ownership of assessment so critical. While administrators provide invaluable support and resources in establishing an assessment structure, it is ultimately the faculty who are responsible for putting findings into action. Their participation, and their leadership, is essential in realizing the full value of assessment for teaching, learning, and student success.

References

Astin, A. W., T. W. Banta, K. P. Cross, E. El-Khawas, P. T. Ewell, P. Hutchings, T. J. Marchese, K. M. McClenney, M. Mentkowski, M. A. Miller, E. T. Moran, and B. D. Wright. 1996. Nine principles of good practice for assessing student learning. Document developed at the American Association of Higher Education Assessment Forum. Available online at *www.cord.edu/ dept/assessment/nineprin.pdf.*

Spellings, M. 2005. *Secretary Spellings announces new commission on the future of higher education.* Press release. Sept. 19. Available online at *www.ed.gov/news/ pressreleases/2005/09/09192005.html.*

Chapter 3

Quantitative Assessment of Student Learning in Large Undergraduate Science Classrooms: Approaches and Caveats

Anneke M. Metz
Department of Cell Biology and Neuroscience
Montana State University
Bozeman, Montana

Introduction: Toward a Reason for Quantitative Assessment

Several years ago, when a group of faculty members in our department was working through a substantial revision of the lower-division biology curriculum, one discussion centered on how we might assess, in a quantitative manner, the effectiveness of our new courses in helping students learn. We were already using a number of assessment tools to solicit student feedback regarding course design, lecture pacing, laboratory exercises, testing strategies, and the like, but the curriculum design group had more direct questions regarding the impact of the new curriculum on the students' knowledge base and skill set.

Because we had no assessment data on the "old" curriculum, save the basic student evaluation forms used by the institution to gauge instructor effectiveness, we were somewhat at a loss for how to begin to gather data to answer important pedagogical questions about newly designed classes. Would it be possible to determine course effectiveness in teaching students basic biological concepts, or to find evidence that inquiry-based laboratories indeed were improving students' analytical or quantitative skills? At a certain point one member of the group pointed out, only half jokingly, that since most of the students were passing the final exam, we already had our evidence that we were teaching students what they needed to know.

I use this anecdote to illustrate a point. In science departments staffed with faculty trained in laboratory science, identifying workable strategies to quantify how and what students learn in the classroom often seems baffling and overwhelming. It also illustrates the need to carefully identify the questions an instructor hopes to answer in a quantitative study of student learning; without such defined study goals, having students perform better on a diagnostic exam at the end of the course than at the beginning, for example, may in and of itself not prove particularly useful in assessing curricular effectiveness. It was difficult for our faculty group, inexperienced in classroom assessment, to move beyond the sense that quantitative assessment performed the same function already covered by giving tests and assigning grades.

Clearly, obtaining detailed, useful assessment data that allows instructors to quantify how and what students learn is no small task. In this chapter, I focus on some of the quantitative assessment work that has been done at Montana State University (MSU) to begin to tease out some of our questions about student learning, particularly in large lower-division biology courses. We have utilized pre- and postcourse administrations of diagnostic instruments, administered weekly quizzes, and tracked engagement with classroom response units ("clickers"). In the process, we have come up with useful, and sometimes surprising, data. Our study results have both validated curricular changes and clarified when course elements did not serve student needs.

Many types of classroom assessment techniques exist, and there is no one strategy that is appropriate for every instance. For an excellent review of approaches to classroom assessment, see Tanner and Allen (2004); the authors reiterate seven basic assumptions of classroom assessment put forth by Angelo and Cross (1993). There are two of those tenets that we have found particularly apropos: (1) "The type of assessment most likely to improve teaching and learning is that conduct-

ed by faculty to answer questions they themselves have formulated in response to issues and problems in their own teaching;" and (2) "classroom assessment does not require specialized training; it can be carried out by dedicated teachers from all disciplines."

These tenets are particularly worth noting for instructors who feel they and their students could benefit from a quantitative assessment of learning outcomes, but who may not have much in the way of assessment expertise at their disposal. There is much to be learned from the literature, and one should never adopt an "anything goes" attitude. However, it is important to realize that even an imperfect assessment is often better than no assessment at all, and it is critical to prevent "assessment paralysis," where the lack of a perfect validated instrument results in no quantitative assessment at all.

At MSU, we have used a variety of strategies to begin to quantitatively assess how students are learning in our science classrooms. It has been extremely helpful as biologists to collaborate with colleagues in physics and astronomy education research, as these disciplines have a rich body of quantitative classroom assessment literature from which to draw. I review in this chapter some of the work that has helped us craft quantitative assessment studies for our biology courses and discuss what we have learned in the process. In doing so, I hope to provide some examples for how other biology faculty not trained in assessment might move toward implementing quantitative assessments in their own classrooms.

Quantitative Assessment of Classroom Methodologies

Generic university assessments are often too broad to pinpoint specific course improvements that could be made by the instructor. However, tailoring assessments to the specific topics and activities of the course can yield specific, meaningful data about what aspects of a course are successful (or are not), and may bring to light some surprising insights. A number of studies quantify student attitudes regarding learning in the biology classroom. The Student Assessment of Learning Gains (SALG) was designed by Seymour, Wiese, and Hunter (2000) to allow students to self-assess their learning in science classrooms. The 46-item SALG instrument uses a 5-point Likert scale, giving students the opportunity to rate the usefulness and effectiveness of lecture and laboratory elements in terms of their own learning.

While not directly testing learning, the instrument does aid in making students more conscious of what they have gained from the course as they reflect on their experience. In addition, as the authors note, aggregate data from student responses allows faculty to identify parts of the course that succeed, and which parts fail, in supporting student learning. The instrument has the benefit of providing qualitative data (individual student comments about course elements) and allowing quantitative analysis (e.g., mean values of Likert-scale responses). The quantitative assessment data can be particularly useful for comparing across sections or course elements. For a case study of how the SALG instrument has been used to assess and improve newly implemented inquiry-based labs in an undergraduate biology curriculum, see Casem (2006).

To gather more nuanced data about how students learn in biology courses, Kitchen et al. (2004) statistically analyzed data from affective assessments. The authors developed instruments to track student feelings about their learning experience, including attitudes toward the material and course design, self-efficacy regarding course content, and sustained intellectual interest in biology. Detailed, quantitative evaluation of the data provided insights into student thinking that would have been difficult to glean otherwise. For example, they found that students evaluated the difficulty of a course differently depending on whether they took an academic stance (an idealistic perspective regarding what a student "should" learn) or a more personal stance (in which they were concerned with the effects of poor performance on their GPA or career goals).

While assessments that ask students to self-assess their perceived level of learning can thus be quite useful in terms of curriculum development, such surveys do not actually test student knowledge of a subject itself. This distinction is important, as there is often a difference between what students *think* they know and what they *actually* know. An excellent example is provided by Bowers, Brandon, and Hill (2005). In this study, students were asked to rate their understanding of biological concepts. Students completed a knowledge survey with 304 content-based questions and were asked to rate how confident they were in their ability to answer each survey item. Students were not required to provide the answers themselves and were given the knowledge survey both at the beginning and end of the semester. There was no correlation between student confidence about their knowledge and actual knowledge itself, as tested by course performance.

At MSU, we have also found a disjunction between student attitudes regarding course difficulty and their actual performance in the same course. Students taking weekly online quizzes in an introductory course evaluated the quizzes as an excessively difficult and unfair component of the course, even when quiz performance correlated very closely with performance in other course components (Metz forthcoming). In contrast to the study of Bowers, Brandon, and Hill (2005), in which students overestimated their understanding of biological concepts, our students underestimated their ability to perform, perhaps because taking quizzes online was unfamiliar to them and caused anxiety. In any event, these studies suggest that student self-assessment of subject knowledge can be either overly optimistic or overly pessimistic, making student attitude surveys problematic as a tool for gauging student learning.

Testing student mastery of specific course concepts requires students to complete a diagnostic instrument. Such instruments most commonly consist of a number of multiple-choice questions, and ideally include foils for each question that allow for the identification of commonly held misconceptions. Students take the pretest at the beginning of the course. The identical posttest instrument is then given at the completion of a course and differences between pre- and posttest scores can be used to calculate learning gains and determine the efficacy of a particular learning tool or environment.

The power of testing learning outcomes via pre- and posttests was made evident via a seminal study performed in physics education research (Hake 1998) in which more than 6,500 physics students at 62 institutions were tested using the Force Concept Inventory (FCI), developed by Hestenes, Wells, and Swackhammer (1992) to gauge student conceptual understanding of elementary mechanics. Student learning of mechanics principles was tested by giving the diagnostic exam both at the beginning and end of the course, and then calculating the average *normalized gain* for students in courses with different teaching strategies. The normalized gain g is defined as the ratio of the actual gain (posttest score minus pretest score) to the maximum possible gain (100% minus pretest score).

In Hake's study, average g values (calculated from coursewide pre- and posttest averages, rather than matched pre- and posttest scores for individual students) were used to compare student performance in traditional physics courses with student performance in courses heavily utilizing "Interactive Engagement" (IE) methods. The traditional courses, consisting of passive lectures, cookbook labs, and rote problem sets, were found to be much less effective pedagogically than IE courses, defined as relying heavily on "heads-on... and hands-on" activities with immediate, personalized feedback and discussion (Hake 1998).

This quantitative analysis of student learning outcomes allowed Hake to show convincingly the positive effect of interactive, personalized instruction at all types of institutions offering introductory physics. The astronomy education research

community has developed a similar instrument for introductory astronomy courses, the Astronomy Diagnostic Test, or ADT (Hufnagel et al. 2000). Like the FCI, the ADT has been used in a number of studies to quantitatively assess student learning (Deming 2002; Zeilik and Morris 2003; and Brogt et al. 2007).

Because normalized gain g is frequently used, particularly in physics/astronomy educational research, it is important to note that this method has some limitations. The normalized gain allows instructors to examine student scores independently of student pretest scores in many instances. However, g can be a problematic measure, as noted by Marx and Cummings (2007). Observed limitations include pretest score bias (see also discussion of learning gains by gender, pp. 20–22), lack of symmetry about the mean for calculated gain scores in a population, and the inability of the formula to handle perfect pretest scores (division by zero error). Marx and Cummings also note students who score lower on the posttest than the pretest can demonstrate relatively large negative g values, which can greatly skew class averages.

As an alternative, Marx and Cummings have devised the *normalized change* value c, which is identical to g when a student's posttest score is higher than the pretest score (the expected and indeed usual outcome). Normalized change then utilizes a score-sensitive strategy to assign c for the three cases that tend to disproportionately skew the gain average: students who score either 0 or 100 on both pre- and posttests (drop score from analysis), students who receive identical pre- and posttest scores (assign $c = 0$), or those who perform worse on the posttest than on the pretest (calculate $c = (post - pre) / pre$). This limits c values to between +1 and -1, and may be a more robust measure to use in populations or course circumstances where a significant number of students do not simply increase their diagnostic test score between pre- and postadministrations.

Taking a cue from the development of instruments such as the FCI and ADT, a number of faculty in biology education research have been developing diagnostic instruments useful for the biology classroom. A development team at the University of Colorado at Boulder has crafted the Biology Concept Inventory, or BCI (Klymkowsky, Garvin-Doxas, and Zeilik 2003; Klymkowsky and Garvin-Doxas 2008; Garvin-Doxas and Klymkowsky 2008). The BCI team has also coordinated efforts of a number of teams working on concept inventories in biology, including genetics, basic biology, evolution and online learning (Garvin-Doxas, Klymkowsky, and Elrod 2007). The BCI itself tests conceptualization of random processes and can be found online at *www.bioliteracy.net*.

Building a sound inventory is an exacting and time-consuming process (for examples on inventory design, see Hestenes, Wells, and Swackhammer 1992; Anderson, Fisher, and Norman 2002; Hufnagel et al. 2000; Garfield 2003; and Garvin-Doxas and Klymkowsky 2008). Despite the availability of these and other carefully developed and validated instruments designed for different subjects, it is often the case that an appropriate instrument for a particular course situation is simply not available. Instructors wishing to answer a specific question about their course may then need to develop their own specific instrument. We have taken this approach in the assessment of several biology courses at MSU.

As part of the redesign of the majors offered in our department (biomedical sciences and cell biology and neuroscience), we reorganized the curriculum to foreground quantitative analysis. One specific goal within the quantitative analysis rubric is increased student competence in the statistical analysis of biological data. Students now take introductory statistics in their first semester, followed by three semesters of introductory biology featuring statistical analysis within inquiry-based laboratory exercises. In assessing this curricular change, we wanted to determine how well students understood certain concepts in statistics after completing an introductory statistics course, and if the use of statistics within the biology courses aided in their understanding and retention of statistical concepts.

Although assessments exist to measure learning in statistics curricula, such as the Statistical Reasoning Assessment (Garfield 2003), there is no instrument available for measuring learning of statistics in a biology curriculum. To this end, we developed a short statistics survey to quantify students' statistical knowledge before and after completing introductory biology (Metz, forthcoming). We designed the survey to touch on statistical knowledge that would be most useful to students using statistics to analyze biological data sets. The questions were also basic enough so that students should have been able to answer all the questions correctly after taking the prerequisite statistics course.

When students took the survey at the start of the introductory biology course, they only averaged 57% correct. Students then completed the biology course, which included emphasis on statistical analysis of biological data sets within the inquiry-based labs, and were then retested with the same survey at the end of the semester. This time, the students averaged 71% correct responses on the posttest (Metz, forthcoming). Our data suggested that the opportunity to practice the use of statistics within a biological context reaffirmed student understanding of the statistics originally learned in a general statistics course. Furthermore, when we retested students one year later, after they had completed two more semesters of biological laboratory with an emphasis on statistical analysis, we found that they retained their understanding of the statistical concepts. Although it could certainly be argued that this instructor-designed instrument has not undergone national testing of reliability and validity and thus has limited use, it nonetheless proved useful for our curriculum development team. By designing a survey instrument to answer a specific question about our curriculum, we were able to gather quantitative evidence that our curriculum fulfilled a specific curricular goal.

As another example, for our second semester introductory biology course, we were interested in assessing students' incoming knowledge of particular biological concepts and in determining the effectiveness of the course itself in teaching these concepts to students. We therefore designed a 34-item instrument specific to the cell biology and genetics material taught in this biology course. Although we have only used this survey in two classes and analysis of the instrument is ongoing, we have used the data gathered so far to compare the performance of men and women in the classroom (see Comparison of Learning Between In-groups and Out-groups, below), and to determine if pretest scores can be used to identify at-risk students (see Assessment as a Tool for Failure Prediction, p. 25). We hope that, eventually, the instrument will have utility in determining the effectiveness of different teaching strategies.

There are other techniques that can be used to quantify learning gains in the classroom besides using a specific instrument, such as a pre- and posttest. Delucchi (2006; 2007) assessed the efficacy of two preparatory procedures in the classroom, weekly quizzes and group projects, in aiding student learning, which was then measured by performance on a final exam. Delucchi statistically analyzed quiz and group project scores for nine years' worth of social statistics courses to calculate the relative contribution of each activity type to student performance on the final. In doing so, he was able to quantify the relative contribution of each activity to student performance in the class.

Student uncertainty about specific course concepts can also be quantified via classroom research. James (2006) has studied how learning takes place in the classroom by recording student conversations during classroom exercises and then scoring and tabulating each student's contribution to the conversation. His work indicates that a high-stakes environment (where students are graded for correct responses in classroom exercises) generates more conversation bias than a low-stakes classroom (where students are graded on participation). By matching a student's course grade to his or her level of domination of the conversation (as measured by number of

ideas put forth as a fraction of all the ideas in the conversation), it became clear that when grades counted, conversations were much less one-sided, and groups were more likely to follow along with a dominant student who was receiving a high grade in the course. A similar approach consisting of observing student groups engaged in in-class learning exercises was used by Adams et al. (2001) to study the gender dynamics of collaborative learning groups in introductory astronomy courses. The researchers found that women were much more likely to be passive in groups that consisted of both males and females, while men's behavior was not affected by the gender composition of the group.

Comparison of Learning Between In-Groups and Out-Groups

As indicated by papers in the literature such as Adams et al. noted above, another question of interest to researchers in science pedagogy is whether particular teaching styles are more effective with certain segments of the classroom population. In other words, do demographic factors such as gender, socioeconomic status, ethic identification or age, to name some common groupings, make a difference in how students learn?

To answer such questions, the same methodology used to compare different pedagogical approaches in the classroom might be considered. Thus, an instructor might administer a pre- and posttest to all students in a course, and then compare the learning gains of different groups of students (for example men and women, or first-generation college students and non-first-generation college students) within the course. However, there is a critical difference between comparing pedagogical approaches, when the student population does not change (study population remains constant while pedagogical approach changes), and comparing different student populations exposed to one pedagogical approach (study population changes while pedagogical approach remains constant). In making this distinction, it is important that we distinguish between two separate quantifiable elements: differences between the performance of student groups being compared on raw pre- or posttest scores, and the learning gains (g or c) calculated for those groups. To make the importance of this distinction clear, it is useful as a case study to examine differences in performance by gender on standardized tests in science, engineering, and mathematics.

Women have historically underperformed on a wide variety of standardized tests in fields in which women have been underrepresented, particularly in the STEM (science, technology, engineering, and mathematics) disciplines. This "performance gap" between men and women is well documented and ongoing (e.g., Wilder and Powell 1989; Cole 1997; Buck, Kostin, and Morgan 2002; McCullough 2004; and Kenney-Benson et al. 2006). The largest differences between men and women can be found on standardized tests of quantitative skills, while both genders have performed similarly on writing and verbal tests since the 1970s. (Women performed somewhat better on written and verbal tests prior to that time.) Tests that continue to show a STEM performance gap between men and women include the Scholastic Aptitude Test (SAT), the Law School Admissions Test (LSAT), the Medical College Admissions Test (MCAT), Advanced Placement (AP) examinations, and the Armed Services Vocational Aptitude Battery (ASVAB). In all these tests, it is the more scientific/quantitative portions of the test in particular that show significantly different performance between males and females (Wilder and Powell 1989).

This gender performance gap is also seen when learning gain instruments are used in college science classrooms. The gender gap on the FCI is about 13% (reported as the difference in normalized gain between men and women by Hake 2002). In national tests of the ADT, men's raw ADT scores average 11–12% higher than women's (Deming 2002). Similarly, men's raw scores on the Force and Motion Concept Evaluation (FMCI) are 11–16% higher than those of their female peers (Pollock, Finkelstein, and Kost 2007).

It is somewhat surprising that this performance gap continues to hold sway to this day, particularly in the biological sciences. Women continue to be underrepresented in physics and mathematics, earning just 21% of undergraduate baccalaureate degrees in physics, 33% in computer science, and 47% in mathematics, in 2000 (NSF 2002). However, in the biological sciences, women have earned 50% or more of the undergraduate biological science degrees since the mid-1990s, having risen steadily from 25% in 1966 (NSF 2002). However, despite the fact that women have achieved parity in the biological sciences at the undergraduate level, this gender performance gap continues to be seen in biology assessments. For instance, the achievement gap on the biological sciences portion of the MCAT has not changed in 30 years: men outperformed women 8.9 to 8.2 on the 2005 MCAT exam, (AAMC 2007), while in 1978, males outscored females 8.6 to 8.0 (Wilder and Powell 1989).

At MSU, we have observed this effect even in courses where the women in the class have equal or higher average GPAs and course grades (Metz, forthcoming). The reasons behind this phenomenon are beyond the scope of this chapter, but scholars have been interested in this question for over 20 years. For an early review of possible reasons—which include biological, social, and psychological explanations, theories of individual differences, and educational variables such as access to education, course-taking patterns, and instruction in specific skills—see Wilder and Powell (1989).

Work in social psychology has focused on the effects of *stereotype threat* and *stereotype lift* in explaining the gender performance gap. Stereotype threat theorizes decreased performance linked to conscious or subconscious fears of affirming the out-group stereotype (e.g., "girls cannot do math"). Conversely, stereotype lift theorizes increased performance relative to a denigrated out-group. For examples of studies that focus on the effect of social stereotyping on standardized test performance, particularly in math and science, see Kenney-Benson et al. 2006; Ritter 2004; and Steele, Spencer, and Aronson 2002.

Raw performance data indicates that the gender performance gap in STEM disciplines is real. However, in studies of classroom learning, normalized gain scores, rather than raw pre- and posttest scores, are widely used to quantify classroom learning, especially since Hake's 1998 study of student learning in the physics classroom (e.g., Coletta and Phillips 2005; Francis, Adams, and Noonan 1998; Lorenzo, Crouch, and Mazur 2006; Pollock, Finkelstein, and Kost 2007; and Hemenway et al. 2002). In these instances, normalized gain is used to focus on student learning in the classroom, regardless of prior knowledge.

Some of these studies have included an examination of performance by different groups of students within the classroom population. Coletta and Phillips (2005) found a positive correlation of FCI prescore and g and found differences in achievement in different learning environments, suggesting that population differences need to be considered in comparing normalized gains between student groups. Other studies have focused directly on the gender performance gap, and have shown normalized gain differences between women and men on the FCI (Lorenzo, Crouch, and Mazur 2006; Hake 2002), FMCI (Pollock, Finkelstein, and Kost 2007), and ADT (Hemenway et al. 2002).

It has recently been demonstrated that the normalized gain index is particularly sensitive to differences in pretest scores (Brogt et al. 2007). The Brogt study utilized three artificial data sets using different learning models to reflect how posttest scores might vary with pretest scores in a classroom situation. Using these generated score pairs to calculate g and then plotting g as a function of the pretest scores indicates that calculated gain values increase exponentially with larger pretest scores. The authors thus suggest that education researchers must approach the use of calculated

learning gains with caution, and calculate gains by several methods to determine if differences between compared groups are robust enough to be seen with multiple gain calculation formulas.

This point becomes crucial in a situation where the groups being compared show significant variation in pretest scores. As an example, in all three learning models, a prescore of 40 results in a normalized gain of 0.3 to 0.4, while a prescore of 60 results in a *doubling* of the calculated normalized gain value (to about 0.6 to 0.8). The calculated g differs even though the "learning" for each individual within the group is equivalent. Because women and men routinely earn different average pretest scores on assessment instruments, we expect women to show lower learning gains than men in classroom learning studies simply because of this fact, rather than any inherent learning differences by gender (Willoughby and Metz 2008).

The lower g values reported for women in physics courses (e.g., Lorenzo, Crouch, and Mazur 2006; Hake 2002) might thus be taken as evidence that women not only perform more poorly on instruments such as pre- and posttests, but also learn less in the courses themselves. However, as we have recently demonstrated for biology and physics courses at MSU, and following the argument of Brogt et al. (2007), calculated learning gain differences between men and women can vary by the gain formula employed (Willoughby and Metz 2008). Educators using a gain measure to assess learning in the classroom are therefore urged to examine carefully any differences in prescores between population groups, and to decide on the appropriate learning gain calculation.

Assessing Learning Via Course Management Systems

Course management systems (CMS) became widely available about a decade ago (Ullman and Rabinowitz 2004). CMS packages such as Web-CT, Blackboard, or Moodle are now ubiquitous on college campuses. At MSU, which has an enrollment of about 11,000 students, more than 800 courses with a CMS component were offered during the 2006–2007 academic year, with 80% of MSU students enrolling in at least one CMS-utilizing course. As these internet-based course content delivery systems become more and more popular, assessment of how they influence student learning is becoming increasingly important.

CMS software can and often is used to deliver distance education (DE) courses, where the entire course is offered online. However, the majority (78%) of courses using CMS at MSU are campus-based. In these courses, the CMS component of the course can be minimal (an online syllabus and student access to their assignment grades) or more complex (online assignments, chat rooms, discussion threads, or other activities). As most of the courses within our department now use CMS to some degree, our faculty members have become particularly interested in the impact of such curricular innovations on student learning.

Luckily, CMS software can easily be set up for student surveys that measure perceptions of learning during or at the end of a course. CMS software allows for anonymous data collection and provides students with the flexibility to access the survey at times convenient to them. We have also found in our biology courses that very modest incentives (some participation points) can result in very high survey completion rates, even when class attendance is relatively low. For these reasons, CMS software is often ideal for collecting student survey data and is often used in our department for this function.

Our experiences in this regard appear similar to other investigators. The SALG survey was shifted from a paper copy to an online survey to streamline the survey process (Seymour, Wiese, and Hunter 2000). The authors point out several advantages to web-administration of a standardized instrument such as the SALG, including saving classroom time, allowing students to complete the survey at their own pace online, and saving

the instructor time in preparing and tabulating paper copies of the survey. This latter point indicates perhaps the greatest advantage of administering surveys online: Data is collected electronically and can be easily tabulated for quantitative analysis.

The impact that CMS has on student learning, when it accompanies a classroom-based undergraduate science course, is under-studied (some examples of studies that quantify effects of online activities as part of a classroom-based course include Freeman et al. 2007; Riffell and Sibley 2005; Riffell, Samuel, and Sibley 2004; and De Souza and Fleming 2003). At the same time, course management systems have enormous potential to allow quantitative assessment of learning. Methods that have already been developed for the quantitative assessment of classroom learning can be adapted for online assignments. For instance, one can imagine that the methodology used by Delucchi (2006; 2007) to track the utility of in-class quizzes on student exam performance could be similarly utilized to examine the impact of online activities, including quizzes, on student learning.

A fascinating aspect of the use of CMS is that it allows educators to examine student patterns of engagement with online course elements. CMS software collects detailed information about how students access course web pages, including how often students view content pages and when and how they complete online assignments. At MSU, analysis of student behavior in the online environment has provided a number of useful insights that we are taking into consideration for future course design. As one example—because most of our biomedical sciences courses use the Web-CT CMS and our faculty are interested in using online systems for weekly quizzes—we are particularly interested in how students utilize online activities, and if they are effective tools for aiding student learning.

We therefore designed studies examining both the patterns of access and performance of students taking online quizzes and doing online homework assignments. In a lower-division biology course where students took weekly quizzes, quiz-taking patterns were analyzed to determine if quiz performance could be used as a predictor of exam performance, or if we would uncover widescale cheating, due to the unsupervised nature of the assignment (Metz, forthcoming). This analysis of online quiz behavior provided some surprising results.

In several of our courses, students were given weekly quizzes online; each student could access the quiz only one time (for 20 minutes) during an access period lasting one to three days. We then tabulated the quiz access times and scores recorded by Web-CT for each student and correlated this data to student course grades. We found that quiz performance correlated quite closely with performance in other course elements, suggesting that quiz grades could be used as an indicator of eventual success in the course. The fact that students did not perform better on online quizzes than on in-class exams also suggested that academic dishonesty was not a large factor in student online performance. Instead, student scores on average decreased over the length of the access period, suggesting that high-performing students were more likely to take online quizzes earlier in the access period and receive high scores. Conversely, struggling students waited until the last minute to take their quiz, as a whole received no help from students who had already completed the quiz, and overall performed more poorly than their peers (Metz, forthcoming).

Because students also had access to these online assignments around the clock, we were interested in studying quiz-taking dynamics. We tabulated the times of day when students took the quiz and found that students were most likely to access quizzes in the late afternoon or early evening. While scores for students taking quizzes during the daytime or early evening hours were similar, we found that scores for quizzes taken after midnight were lower by a statistically significant degree. Again, the insights we have made into how our students engage with the course material, made possible by quantitative analysis of student performance, will allow us to make better decisions about how

to structure course assignments with CMS.

As a second example, an analysis of how students accessed online homework via Web-CT has proved enlightening in terms of how an instructor might best structure online assignments. In the spring of 2008, students in an upper-division cell biology course were required to complete weekly, 10–20 question, multiple-choice homework assignments via Web-CT. The students were given unlimited access to alleviate the stress students had experienced with one-time access quizzes in previous courses, and also to give students free reign to utilize the homework to maximize their learning. Questions were worth one point each, and upon submission, each student received the total score, but not the answers, for the homework. Students could then choose to re-access the assignment as many times as they wished to improve their score, with the best score counting as their assignment grade at the end of the access period. The access period for each homework assignment was one week, and homework overall counted for 25% of the final grade for the course (the other 75% consisted of in-class exams).

We had hoped that in an upper-division course with difficult exams, students would use homework assignments as an opportunity to test themselves on course material. Because Web-CT records the details of each student attempt (access time, length of access, questions answered, and the total score for the attempt), we were able to track how each student arrived at their final homework score. Under this generous set of access rules—where students could take as much time as they wished, use lecture notes or the course text to find answers, and try again if they did not get a perfect score—we were disappointed to find that students did not use the homework assignments at all to learn course material. Instead, students in the class very quickly learned that they could simply submit the homework after completing only one question, and in this way determine the correct answer for each question by trial and error (by checking if they received a score of "1"). *Every* student in the course resorted to "video-gaming" their way to a perfect

TABLE 1. Correlations of pretest scores to final grades in three biology courses at MSU.

N= sample size; r = Pearson's correlation coefficient. R2 indicates proportion of a student's grade that can be accounted for by performance on the pretest.

Course	N	r	R2
Introductory Biology I	213	0.323	10.5%
Introductory Biology II	186	0.205	3.7%
Advanced Cell Biology	71	0.504	24.3%

homework score. *No* student even attempted to use the homework as a learning exercise (Metz, unpublished data). This quantitative analysis indicates that given too much latitude to discover correct answers without needing to engage with course content, students in this particular course chose an easy mechanistic approach to earning points.

These example are instructive because they illustrate the utility of CMS software in quantifying both student performance and learning behavior. Because CMS so exhaustively document access times, duration of access, student responses, and other aspects of assignment completion, instructors now also have the ability to quantitatively assess student behavior patterns as well as student performance data. This type of data will help instructors better tailor their course assignments to maximize student learning.

Assessment as a Tool for Failure Prediction

If one of the concerns of the quantitative assessment of classroom learning is to improve engagement of those students who appear not to be served by traditional methods, identification of students who are most likely to fail is paramount. Freeman et al. (2007) performed a risk analysis to determine if there were available measures that accurately predict low course performance in an introductory biology course at the University of

Washington. After examining the achievement of more than 3,000 students, it was found that student GPAs at the institution and verbal SAT scores were the most reliable predictors of success in the course. This information was used to generate a mathematical model utilizing these predictors. Students were considered "high risk" for failure if they were predicted to receive a 2.5 or lower (on a 4.0 scale) in the course using the model. Having a predictive model allows instructors to target students at risk for failure for interventions, if resources are available. More generally, such analyses can show the benefits of structuring courses in a way that retains more of these students.

Hake returned to the large data set used to examine differences between traditional classrooms and courses utilizing IE methodologies (1998) to search for variables within student populations that might be useful in predicting which students are more likely to achieve lower gains in a physics course (2002). Although he tested math skills and spatial visualization ability and examined high school preparation (in this case high school physics) and FCI pretest scores, none of these were more than weakly correlated with low *g*; it may be necessary instead to consider multiple variables to identify at-risk students as Freeman et al. (2007) found.

Chapman, Christmann, and Thatcher (2006) used a 30-item diagnostic pretest designed by the authors to identify students in need of remediation in an undergraduate bioinformatics course.

The impetus was to determine if lack of prerequisite knowledge correlated with the likelihood of the student dropping the course. This study is particularly noteworthy because the authors looked specifically at reasons why students dropped the course. The pretest consisted of six areas of prerequisite knowledge needed for a bioinformatics course, including chemistry, computing, evolution, "web-savvy" (comfort level using internet-based tools), mathematics, and molecular biology, allowing the authors to determine what prerequisite knowledge in particular had the greatest effect on students' ability to complete the course. Interestingly, they found that an understanding of molecular biology, rather than computing or web experience, had the greatest impact on retention for this computing-heavy course. This alone demonstrates the surprising curricular insights that can be found through quantitative analysis.

At MSU, our biology faculty are also interested in finding models that can help identify students who may be at risk for doing poorly in, or failing, a course. Toward this end, we have examined the correlations between pretests and final grades in three different large-enrollment courses. So far, we have found that the survey instrument had only weak predictive power for student achievement (see Table 1 p. 25); we have therefore not yet found a survey appropriate to our courses to serve as a useful instrument for identifying at-risk students. Once again, it appears likely that a model using multiple variables, as demonstrated by Freeman et al. (2007) will be required to effectively identify struggling students at the start of a course.

A Note About Capturing "Strugglers"

One issue of concern in the quantitative assessment of student learning, particularly in large-lecture courses, is any study's ability to capture the student "strugglers." These are the students who will eventually receive barely passing grades, fail the course, or withdraw from the course late in the term to avoid a poor grade. We have found in our large-lecture biology courses that struggling students are disproportionately absent from lectures, compared to their student peers who are doing well in the course. They are also much less likely to complete online assignments and sit for examinations. This effect grows more pronounced near the end of the course, precisely when posttest diagnostic instruments are administered in learning-gain studies. Struggling students are thus disproportionately excluded from many classroom studies.

Few classroom studies in undergraduate biology education have specifically examined the performance of students who eventually fail to complete a course. The study performed by Chapman, Christmann, and Thatcher (2006) is one example in which the investigators looked specifically at how student performance on different classes of questions correlated with their likelihood of dropping the course. Their work suggests that test results of the students who drop a course may differ markedly from test results of students who complete a course.

In studies where learning gains are being studied via a pre- and posttest design, capturing the maximum number of students is necessary to get the most complete picture of student achievement. However, as noted above, the students who are struggling are less likely than their peers to complete posttest assessments (Metz, forthcoming). A common technique to gather posttest data is simply to have students complete the instrument as an in-class activity on one of the last days of the semester. Depending on the nature of the study or the instrument, this may be considered by the instructor to be the fairest way to gather this data, and we have ourselves used this tactic at MSU. However, in quantitative assessment studies performed in physics (S. Willoughby, personal communication) and biology courses at Montana State University, giving posttests as ungraded, unannounced in-class exercises near the end of the semester results in very low response rates (around 60%).

We were able to increase the participation rate

to about 80% for a posttest in a lower-division biology course by notifying students in advance that there would be an in-class activity worth 5 participation points. We have seen other evidence that point incentives make a difference in the rate of participation in class activities. Thus, while attendance rates in our large first- and second-year biology courses where no grade incentive is provided for course attendance averages about 60% near the end of the semester, attendance in these same courses stays near 80% when daily attendance points are awarded via Classroom Response Systems (individual student "clickers").

As noted by Freeman et al. (2007), it is likely that the students who struggle most or who fail to complete courses are also the ones who are likely to benefit most from methods in the classroom that increase student engagement. It is therefore critical to consider ways in which we can ensure participation of these students in any classroom study. A number of strategies may be used to encourage higher posttest completion rates for these students. Multiple administrations of the posttest may increase participation, but this strategy also introduces confounding variables, since testing conditions can no longer be said to be identical for all students. Having students take posttests as an online exercise may similarly provide better participation by a larger percentage of the enrolled students, but may give the instructor even less control of the conditions under which students are tested.

We have found that embedding the posttest instrument in the final exam or other graded exercise late in the semester has several advantages. It both captures every (or nearly every) student who will complete the course, and it strongly encourages students to take the instrument seriously (in our experience, an ongoing problem when students are not graded on exercises administered late in the semester). This embedding strategy has allowed us to capture 92% of enrolled students in one study over two semesters in an introductory biology course at MSU, with the only students not completing the assessment being those who dropped the course late in the term. How-ever, embedding the instrument in an exam may not be appropriate and is thus not an option in all instances. Finally, although embedding the assessment in a final exam guarantees that students who complete the course are assessed, it still does not capture students who drop late in the term or simply stop coming to class near the end of the semester.

Conclusions

Although we certainly have not come close to answering every question about how and what students learn, it has been gratifying to begin to glean some answers about classroom dynamics and about pedagogical interventions that make a difference in our biology courses at MSU. All educators who are interested in learning more about the dynamics of their classrooms and would like to know if a new teaching strategy has effectively increased student understanding of the subject should be encouraged to engage in quantitative assessment of classroom learning.

The use of surveys that can quantify student attitudes of the learning environment, and that can quantify student self-assessment of learning gains, often provides critical insight for course development. However, assessing actual learning gains provides data beyond student perceptions about what students are learning. Such data, whether gained via pre- and posttesting, by looking at the effect of different course activities on final course performance, or by other means, can prove extremely useful in finding teaching strategies that work. The quantification of learning gains is especially important because it is clear that student perceptions about their own understanding and actual performance may not be the same (Bowers, Brandon, and Hill 2005; Metz, forthcoming).

Finally, there are some considerations worth keeping in mind in designing learning gain studies. When comparing student populations, it is critical to consider the possible effects of stereotype threat and stereotype lift in study design, particularly if a gain calculation sensitive to average pretest score, such as the normalized gain, is used to compare in- and out-groups. Finding ways to maximize participation of struggling students will likewise result in a fuller data set that will allow curricular interventions to be made that benefit all students in the classroom. With these caveats in mind, the quantitative assessment of learning outcomes in undergraduate science classrooms is a worthwhile undertaking. Such studies, performed either independently or in conjunction with more traditional forms of classroom assessment, can provide the kind of detailed, rich evaluative data needed to make excellent education possible.

References

Adams, J. P., G. Brissenden, R. S. Lindell, T. F. Slater, and J. Wallace. 2001. Observations of student behavior in collaborative learning groups. *Astronomy Education Review* 1 (1): 8.

Anderson, D. L., K. M. Fisher, and G. J. Norman. 2002. Development and evaluation of the conceptual inventory of natural selection. *Journal of Research in Science Teaching* 39 (10): 952–978.

Angelo, T.A., and K. P. Cross. 1993. *Classroom assessment techniques: A handbook for college teachers.* San Francisco, CA: Jossey-Bass.

Association of American Medical Colleges (AAMC). 2007. Medical college admissions test: Characteristics of examinees and summary data. Available online at *www.aamc. org/students/mcat/examineedata/pubs.htm*.

Bowers, N., M. Brandon, and C. D. Hill. 2005. The use of a knowledge survey as an indicator or student learning in an introductory biology course. *CBE—Life Sciences Education* 4: 311–322.

Brogt E., D. Sabers, E. E. Prather, G. E. Deming, B. Hufnagel, and T. F. Slater. 2007. Analysis of the astronomy diagnostic test. *Astronomy Education Review* 6 (1): 25–42.

Buck, G., I. Kostin, and R. Morgan. 2002. Examining the relationship of content to gender-based performance differences in advanced placement exams. *College board research report no. 2002-12.* New York: The College Board.

Casem, M. L. 2006. Student perspectives on curricular change: Lessons from an undergraduate lower-division biology core. *CBE—Life Sciences Education* 5: 65–75.

Chapman, B. S., J. L. Christmann, and E. F. Thatcher. 2006. Bioinformatics for undergraduates: Steps toward a quantitative bioscience curriculum. *Biochemistry and Molecular Biology Education* 34 (3): 180–186.

Cole, N. S. 1997. *The ETS gender study: How females and males perform in educational settings.* Princeton, NJ: Educational Testing Service.

Coletta, V. P., and J. A. Phillips. 2005. Interpreting FCI scores: Normalized gain, preinstruction scores, and scientific reasoning ability. *American Journal of Physics* 73 (12): 1172–1182.

Delucchi, M. 2006. The efficacy of collaborative learning groups in an undergraduate statistics course. *College Teaching* 54 (2): 244–248.

Delucchi, M. 2007. Assessing the impact of group projects on examination performance in social statistics. *Teaching in Higher Education* 12 (4): 447–460.

Deming, G. L. 2002. Results of the astronomy diagnostic test national project. *Astronomy Education Review* 1 (1): 52–57.

De Souza, E., and M. Fleming. 2003. A comparison of in-class and on-line quizzes on student exam performance. *Journal of Computing in Higher Education* 14 (2): 121–134.

Francis, G. E., J. P. Adams, and E. J. Noonan. 1998. Do they stay fixed? *The Physics Teacher* 36: 488–490.

Freeman, S., E. O'Connor, J. W. Parks, M. Cunningham, D. Hurley, D. Haak, C. Dirks, and M. P. Wenderoth. 2007. Prescribed active learning increases performance in introductory biology. *CBE—Life Sciences Education* 6: 132–139.

Garfield, J. B. 2003. Assessing statistical reasoning. *Statistical Education Research Journal* 2 (1): 22–38.

Garvin-Doxas, K., and M. Klymkowsky. 2008. Understanding randomness and its impact on student learning: Lessons learned from building the biology concept inventory (BCI). *CBE—Life Sciences Education* 7.

Garvin-Doxas, K., M. Klymkowsky, and S. Elrod. 2007. Building, using and maximizing the impact of concept inventories in the biological sciences: Report on a National Science Foundation-sponsored conference on the construction of concept inventories in the biological sciences. *CBE—Life Science Education* 6: 277–282.

Hake, R. R. 1998. Interactive-engagement versus traditional methods: A six thousand-student survey of mechanics test data for introductory physics courses. *American Journal of Physics* 66 (1): 67–74.

Hake, R. R. 2002. Relationship of individual student normalized learning gains in mechanics with gender, high-school physics, and pretest scores on mathematics and spatial visualization. Paper submitted to the Physics Education Research Conference, Boise, Idaho. Available online at *www.physics.indiana.edu/~hake/PERC2002h-Hake.pdf*.

Hemenway, M. K., W. J. Straits, R. R. Wilke, and B. Hufnagel. 2002. Educational research in an introductory astronomy course. *Innovative Higher Education* 26 (4): 271–280.

Hestenes, D., M. Wells, and G. Swackhammer. 1992. Force concept inventory. *Physics Teacher* 30: 141–158.

Hufnagel, B, T. Slater, G. L. Deming, J. Adams, R. L. Adrian, C. Brick, and M. Zeilik. 2000. Pre-course results from the astronomy diagnostic test. *Electronic Publications of the Astronomy Society of Australia* 17 (2). Available online at *www.atnf.csiro.au/pasa/17_2*.

James, M. C. 2006. The effect of grading incentive on student discourse in peer instruction. *American Journal of Physics* 74 (8): 689–691.

Kenney-Benson, G. A., E. M. Pomerantz, A. M. Ryan, and H. Patrick. 2006. Sex differences in math performance: The role of children's approach to schoolwork. *Developmental Psychology* 42 (1): 11–26.

Kitchen, E., S. Reeve, J. D. Bell, R. R. Sudweeks, and W. S. Bradshaw. 2004. The development of affective assessment in an upper-level cell biology course. *Journal of Research in Science Teaching* 44 (8): 1057–87.

Klymkowsky, M. W., and K. Garvin-Doxas. 2008. Recognizing student misconceptions through Ed's Tools and the biology concept inventory. *PLoS Biology* 6 (1): e3.

Klymkowsky, M. W., K. Garvin-Doxas, and M. Zeilik. 2003. Bioliteracy and teaching efficacy: What biologists can learn from physicists. *Cell Biology Education* 2: 155–161.

Lorenzo, M., C. H. Crouch, and E. Mazur. 2006. Reducing the gender gap in the physics classroom. *American Journal of Physics* 74 (2): 118–122.

Marx, J. D., and K. Cummings. 2007. Normalized change. *American Journal of Physics* 75 (1): 87–91.

McCullough, L. 2004. Gender, context, and physics assessment. *Journal of International Women's Studies* 5 (4): 20–30.

Section

1

Metz, A. M. Forthcoming. The effect of access time on on-line quiz performance in large biology lecture courses. *Biochemistry and Molecular Biology Education.*

Metz, A.M. Forthcoming. Teaching statistics in biology: Using inquiry-based learning to strengthen understanding of statistical analysis in biology laboratory courses. *CBE—Life Sciences Education.*

National Science Foundation (NSF), Division of Resource Statistics. 2002. *Science and engineering degrees, 1966–2000.* NSF 02-327. Available online at *www.nsf.gov/statistics/nsf02327.*

Pollock, S. J., N. D. Finkelstein, and L. E. Kost. 2007. Reducing the gender gap in the physics classroom: How sufficient is interactive engagement? *Physical Review Special Topics—Physics Education Research* 3: 010107-1–010107-4.

Riffell, S. K., K. Samuel, and D. F. Sibley. 2004. Can hybrid course formats increase attendance in undergraduate science courses? *Journal of Natural Resources and Life Sciences Education* 33: 16–20.

Riffell, S. K., and D. F. Sibley. 2005. Using web-based instruction to improve large undergraduate biology courses: An evaluation of a hybrid course format. *Computers & Education* 44: 217–235.

Ritter, D. 2004. Gender role orientation and performance of stereotypically feminine and masculine cognitive tasks. *Sex Roles* 50 (7/8): 583–591.

Seymour, E., D. J. Wiese, and A. Hunter. 2000. Creating a better mousetrap: On-line student assessment of their learning gains. Paper presented to the National Meetings of American Chemical Society Symposium. San Francisco, March 27, 2000.

Steele, C. M., S. J. Spencer, and J. Aronson. 2002. Contending with group image: The psychology of stereotype and social identity threat. In *Advances in Experimental Social Psychology Vol. 34,* ed. M. Zanna, 329–340. New York: Academic Press.

Tanner, K., and D. Allen. 2004. Approaches to biology teaching and learning: From assays to assessments—on collecting evidence in science teaching. *Cell Biology Education* 3: 69–74.

Ullman, C., and M. Rabinowitz. 2004. Course management systems and the reinvention of instruction. *T.H.E. Journal.* Available online at *http://thejournal.com/articles/17014.*

Wilder, G. Z., and K. Powell. 1989. *Sex differences in test performance: A survey of the literature.* College Board Report No. 89-3. New York: College Entrance Examination Board.

Willoughby, S. D., and A. Metz. 2008. Inherent gender bias in learning gain calculations for introductory physics and biology courses. Submitted for publication.

Zeilik, M., and V. J. Morris. 2003. An examination of misconceptions in an astronomy course for science, mathematics, and engineering majors. *Astronomy Education Review* 1 (2): 101.

Chapter 4

Means of Linking Research to Practice in Organizing a Course on Student Assessment

HsingChi von Bergmann
Faculty of Education
University of Calgary
Calgary, AB, Canada

Accurate assessment of student achievement is an important requirement of educators. In my role as professor in Science Education at the University of Calgary, I have taught an assessment course for master's students and student teachers for several semesters. Over that time I have found it most appropriate to organize the course in four major areas: Assessment for Learning, Assessment for Instruction, Assessment for Accountability, Assessment for Reflection. The following description is how the course progresses through the semester.

In the first part of the course, students are exposed to learning theories, particularly on cognitive psychologists' studies around higher-order thinking skills to understand various ways of assessment for understanding. The students are asked to construct several multiple-choice items in their specific discipline and for a specific age group. The items are designed to assess students' higher-order cognitive skills rather than just knowledge. With this activity and discussions on characteristics of good multiple-choice items, they understand the limitations of multiple-choice questions. Students are then introduced to authentic assessments and the design and usage of rubrics. The assignment for them is to develop authentic assessment and evaluation rubrics in their chosen discipline for a specific age group of students.

In the second part of the course, students are exposed to questioning literature to understand what effective questioning practices are and how questioning can assist classroom diagnostic skills of teachers to modify instruction. Specifically they discuss divergent versus convergent question types, and the strengths and weaknesses of these questions. The assignment is to develop a set of questions they will use when they interview a couple of students and write up what instructional modifications they will make to address students' preconceptions. With the reading by Black and Wiliam (1998), providing feedback to students and parents is identified as one major topic for classroom assessment in the course.

In the third part of the course, students are introduced to large-scale assessment and what role it plays in education. The issues of designing large-scale assessment, the criterion-based or norm-referenced assessment, what validity and reliability are in test design, the use of the result, and the impacts it has on classroom teachers are explored. Subsequently students are introduced to reporting and grading issues. Methodological issues involved in ranking schools using large-scale assessment results were also discussed in this part of the class. We closed this section of the course using Kifer's (2001) Large-Scale Assessment Grid to evaluate examples of large-scale assessment, such as provincial standardized tests, NAEP, PISA, and TIMSS.

For the last part of the course, literature focuses on metacognition and how it plays a role for individual learners to develop deep understanding in both disciplinary areas and their own learning process. Students in this course are asked to submit a learning e-portfolio to represent their own learning in this course. Reflection is one of the categories students must include in their e-portfolio. Students collectively develop the evaluation rubrics for the e-portfolio earlier in the semester for the instructor to assess their learning.

I did not have a course outline for the course. Instead, I list the topics (course objectives) that will be introduced in the course. In the first class I often let my students do a need-assessment exercise after introducing the learning objectives.

They then determine the topics they most need and decide on the sequence of the course topics. The resulting sequence over the past two years has been what is described here. According to your own educational context, perhaps your students will have a different set of needs that will result in a different sequence.

The books I recommended to the students of the course are

Dantonio, M., and P. C. Beisenherz. 2000. *Learning to question, questioning to learn: Developing effective teacher questioning practices.* Columbus, OH: Allyn & Bacon.

Guskey, T. R. 2003. *How's my kid doing? A parent's guide to grades, marks, and report cards.* San Francisco, CA: Jossey-Bass.

Guskey, T. R., and J. M. Bailey. 2000. *Developing grading and reporting systems for student learning.* Thousand Oaks, CA: Corwin Press.

Kifer, E. 2001. *Large-scale assessment: Dimensions, dilemmas, and policy.* Thousand Oaks, CA: Corwin Press.

Kleinert, H. L., and J. F. Kearns. 2001. *Alternate assessment: Measuring outcomes and supports for students with disabilities.* Baltimore, MD: Brookes.

Wiggins, G. P. 1993. *Assessing student performance: Exploring the purpose and limits of testing.* San Francisco, CA: Jossey-Bass.

The articles I recommended to students of the course are

Baker, E. L. 2007. The end(s) of testing. *Educational Researcher* 36: 309–317.

Black, P., and D. Wiliam. 1998. Assessment and classroom learning. *Assessment in Education: Principles, Policy & Practice* 5 (1): 7–75.

SECTION 2

Assessment in the College Classroom

Chapter 5

Writing/Using Multiple-Choice Questions to Assess Higher-Order Thinking

Kerry L. Cheesman
Biological Sciences
Capital University
Columbus, Ohio

Introduction

Multiple-choice exams are widely used in college science classrooms (as well as for laboratory quizzes and exams). Multiple-choice questions have many advantages—perhaps the most important is that they can be graded quickly and easily, and they can be graded by either human or machine. The "clicker" systems often used in large lecture rooms are well adapted for answering multiple-choice questions, and they can be used for "instant quizzes" with immediate feedback to students.

Instructor time is valuable, and in large classrooms the use of essay exams (the primary alternative) can quickly become overwhelming, causing students to wait for feedback for prolonged periods of time. Feedback on progress needs to be as rapid as possible, and essay questions do not lend themselves to that. Essay grading can also tend to be biased by any number of factors (time of day, personal biases, differences between graders, lack of openness to new interpretations, and so on).

Finally, most graduate entrance exams (including the GRE, MCAT, and DAT) are based on multiple-choice questions. Many later exams, such as the medical board exams, are also multiple-choice. Therefore, it is important to make sure that students are prepared for higher-order multiple-choice exams and the reasoning that is required to answer the questions in a proficient manner. Undergraduate science instructors can help students be well prepared by using higher-order multiple-choice questions for assessment of course material starting in the freshman year.

Assessment must match one's teaching style—inquiry teaching must be followed by assessment techniques that match the inquiry method of teaching. If one follows the learning cycle (5E or other similar models), assessment is encountered throughout the teaching and learning continuum, and that assessment must be related to the phase of the cycle (exploration, extension, etc.). Certainly higher-order questions capture the essence of exploration and extension much better than lower-order questions do.

The use of higher-order questions does not mean an end to using lower-order questions. Rather, we are referring to a shift from the t 80–90% lower-order questions typically found in college science exams toward a balance between lower- and higher-order questions. The goal of undergraduate science instruction should be critical thinking rather that memorization. Many students come to the university with the assumption that science is just a lot of memorization, and college instructors often need to work hard to destroy that myth. However, that myth is often kept alive by the choice of questions used on the exams. If they favor knowledge-style questions, then students will continue to believe that science is mostly about memorization rather than about inquiry and analysis.

Understanding Bloom's Taxonomy

Most college instructors are familiar, on some level, with Bloom's taxonomy of learning (Bloom et al. 1956). Much has been written about the use of Bloom's taxonomy in the construction of exam questions, but few instructors take to heart the need to use all of the levels instead of just the first two in constructing examination questions. Here is a quick review of Bloom's taxonomy as it relates to the teaching of college science.

1. Knowledge: the ability to remember/recall previously learned material.

>*Examples of behavioral verbs:* list, name, identify, define, show

>*Sample learning objectives in science:* know common terms, know specific facts, know basic procedures and methods

2. Comprehension (understanding): the ability to grasp the meaning of material, and to explain or restate ideas.

>*Examples of behavioral verbs:* chart, compare, contrast, interpret, demonstrate

>*Sample learning objectives in science:* understand facts and principles, interpret charts and graphs, demonstrate laboratory methods and procedures

3. Application: the ability to use learned material in new situations.

>*Examples of behavioral verbs:* construct, manipulate, calculate, illustrate, solve

>*Sample learning objectives in science:* apply concepts and principles to new situations, apply theories to practical situations, construct graphs and charts

4. Analysis: the ability to separate material into component parts and show relationships between the parts.

>*Examples of behavioral verbs:* classify, categorize, organize, deduce, distinguish

>*Sample learning objectives in science:* distinguish between facts and inferences, evaluate the relevancy of data, recognize unstated assumptions

5. Synthesis: the ability to put together separate ideas to form a new whole or establish new relationships.

>*Examples of behavioral verbs:* hypothesize, create, design, construct, plan

>*Sample learning objectives in science:* propose a plan for an experiment, formulate a new scheme for classifying, integrate multiple areas of learning into a plan to solve a problem

6. Evaluation: the ability to judge the worth or value of material against stated criteria.

> *Examples of behavioral verbs:* evaluate, recommend, criticize, defend, justify
>
> *Sample learning objective in science:* judge the way that conclusions are supported by the data

It is a common misconception that as one climbs the scale of Bloom's taxonomy, the difficulty of the questions increases. The increase in cognitive demand associated with higher-order questions refers to the *complexity* of the questions, not the difficulty. Higher-order questions require a different set of cognitive demands, but they are not necessarily more difficult.

Writing Multiple Choice Questions

Higher order multiple choice questions can be as easy or as difficult to construct as lower-order questions. Good-quality questions are essential to being able to truly assess a student's knowledge and understanding of the subject matter in any area of science.

Before attempting to construct individual questions, think about the purpose of the questions. In general, the purpose should be to assess what students know and don't know, and how students are able to construct knowledge based on prior learning. Therefore, avoid "trick" questions that may confuse students who understand the material. Avoid using prepared test banks written by the author of the textbook or other contracted writers. Honest assessment *must* match the teaching style employed, not the style of the textbook or the style of your colleagues. Note: You cannot ask higher-order questions if your teaching style mandates only recall.

Writing good multiple-choice questions takes time—a well-constructed test can't be written in a single day. Questions need to be written, reviewed for clarity, and often revised. Questions need to be constructed in such a way that they neither re-ward test-wise students nor penalize those whose test-taking skills are less developed. The purpose is to assess student learning, and therefore each question needs to be clearly designed to achieve that goal. Remember that higher-order questions take longer to answer than recall questions, so plan accordingly in the construction of the test.

To construct a higher-order multiple-choice question, start by constructing the stem. The stem should pose a problem or state a question. Familiar forms include case study, premise and consequence, problem and solution, incomplete scenario, and analogy. The stem may involve pictures and diagrams or just words.

Write the stem as clearly and simply as possible. A student should be able to understand the problem without having to read it several times. Always try to state the problem in a positive form, as students often misread negatively phrased questions. Avoid extraneous language that is irrelevant to the question. While some authors believe this helps separate those who truly understand from those who don't, too often it confuses even the well-prepared students, leading to unreliability of the question.

Never use double negatives. Avoid "which of these is the *best* choice" unless that format is integral to the learning objectives. Be sure to include in the stem any words that are redundant to all of the answers, and use "a(n)" or "a/an" to avoid eliminating any of the answers as mismatches.

Once the stem is constructed, proceed with writing the responses. Write the correct answer first. This allows you to be sure it is well constructed and accurate, and allows you to match the remaining answers to it. Avoid verbal cues, and certainly avoid lifting phrases directly from the text or class notes. Be sure that the incorrect responses match the correct one in length, complexity, phrasing, and style. For instance, in the following example, the mismatch of the answers makes it easy to guess the correct response even if one has little knowledge of the subject material.

The term "side effect of a drug":
a. refers to any action of a drug in the body

other than the one the doctor wanted the drug to have

b. is the main effect of a drug

c. additionally benefits the individual

Distracters (incorrect answers) must be incorrect yet plausible. If a recognizable key word appears in the correct answer, it should appear in some of the distracters as well. Be sure to check—will the answers help to distinguish *why* a student got it wrong? This is an important part of assessment that is often overlooked by instructors, but is a critical part of helping students to learn.

Avoid microscopic distinctions between answers, unless this is a significant objective of the course. Be sure to stagger the correct responses in their order (use all answer positions as equally as possible). Limit the number of options—most authors agree that 4–5 answers is plenty, and there is no assessment advantage in using more than five. Use *all, always, never, none,* etc., rarely. These are answers that students have been programmed to

shy away from and may distort the question as a valid assessment tool. Likewise, use *all of the above* and *none of the above* sparingly.

When all exam questions have been constructed, check each one to see where it falls in Bloom's hierarchy. Construct a simple table such as that shown in Table 1 to see the distribution of questions. If the questions are disproportionately distributed, then rewrite enough questions to balance the exam between lower-order and higher-order questions.

Examples of Multiple-Choice Questions at Each Level

The following examples illustrate the construction of multiple-choice questions that fit the higher levels of Bloom's taxonomy. For most an explanation is included describing why it fits where it does, and what a student needs to know to be able to answer the question correctly.

TABLE 1. Sample table showing the distribution of questions

Topics/ Objectives	Recall (knowledge, comprehension)	Application (application, analysis)	Evaluation (synthesis, evaluation)	%
a.				
b.				
c.				
d.				
e.				
f.				
Total				

Application Questions

1. Susie and Bill are both healthy and have healthy parents. Each of them has a sister with *autosomal recessive cystic fibrosis*. If Susie and Phil have a child, what is the probability that it will be born with cystic fibrosis?
   a. 0
   b. 2/3
   c. 1/2
   d. 1/4
   e. 1/9

(To answer this question correctly, one must understand the terms *autosomal* and *recessive*, and also understand the concepts of probability as applied to human genetics. In this question the student must apply those concepts to a family situation not studied before. The incorrect responses are constructed to find misconceptions/misunderstandings about genetic probabilities.)

2. A total of 100 students at Capital University were tested for blood type. The results showed 36 were type O, 28 were type A, 28 were type B, and 8 were type AB. The frequency of the A allele is therefore:
   a. 0.10
   b. 0.14
   c. 0.28
   d. 0.56
   e. 0.64

(To answer correctly, a student must know the formula for allele frequency and be able to calculate it from the given data. The answers were chosen to help find misunderstandings about allele frequency.)

3. Evolutionary forces have produced an unusual plant, the Indian Pipe, that has no chlorophyll. Therefore, the plant must:
   a. make its own food
   b. absorb food made by other organisms
   c. photosynthesize without chlorophyll
   d. respire without taking in food
   e. use chlorophyll from other plants

(To answer this question the role of chlorophyll in energy transformation must be understood. The student must apply the concepts of energy transformation/lack of chlorophyll to a logical new endpoint. All of the answers are plausible and help to distinguish where an understanding of energy transformation is incomplete.)

4. Which of the following compounds should have the highest boiling point?
   a. $CH_3CH_2CH_2CH_3$
   b. CH_3NH_2
   c. CH_3OH
   d. CH_2F_2

(To answer correctly, a student must understand the concept of boiling point and the role of various constituent chemical groups in raising or lowering the boiling point.)

Analysis Questions

1. When a solid ball is added to a graduated cylinder with water in it, the water level rises from 20 ml to 50 ml. What is the volume of the ball?
   a. 20 ml
   b. 30 ml
   c. 50 ml
   d. 70 ml

(In this example, a student must understand the concept of volume and not get distracted by the spherical nature of the added object. The answers are designed to give the instructor a sense of the misunderstanding of volume.)

2. From the graph shown here, determine when maximal carrying capacity has been reached.
   a. point A on the graph
   b. point B on the graph
   c. point C on the graph
   d. point D on the graph

(To answer correctly a student must be able to see the relationships among the various organisms, interpret those relationships, and evaluate the ecosystem relative to the organisms shown on the graph.)

3. During an otherwise normal pregnancy, a woman begins to experience light-headedness and a decline in energy levels near the end of the first trimester. Which of the following is the most likely cause of her symptoms?

a. lack of B vitamins due to poor diet

b. decline of blood pH due to overuse of muscles

c. decrease in blood pressure due to expanding fetal circulation

d. decline in estrogen levels due to ovarian shutdown

(All of these answers involve factors that could cause tiredness in a woman. To determine the most likely cause in this scenario, a student needs to understand the basic mechanics of pregnancy and the biochemical changes that occur during it. The answer given shows a student's ability to carefully analyze the situation and determine causality.)

4. The seeds of various plants vary in size from a fraction of a millimeter to several centimeters. The most critical factor controlling the size seed a plant produces is

a. size of the maternal flower

b. projected size of the animal pollinator

c. quantity of the abiotic pollinator

d. length of predicted dormancy

e. method of distribution of seed

Synthesis Questions

1. Domoic acid, produced by diatoms, has been found to bind to hippocampal glutamate receptors. If a person were to accidentally consume a lot of shellfish contaminated with this organism, what effect might be expected?

a. blindness

b. deafness

c. amnesia

d. aphasia

e. rigidity

(To answer this question, one must understand the role of the hippocampus and the role of glutamate in this area of the brain. Here a stu-

dent's knowledge of the brain is used to establish a new relationship beyond those studied in class. All of the answers are logical outcomes of brain dysfunction and help the instructor to pinpoint the misunderstandings that students have.)

2. A neighbor found some mammal bones on the ground—a keeled sternum and an ulna, where the olecranon occupies 30% of the length of the bone. These bones most likely came from what type of mammal?

a. flyer

b. climber

c. runner

d. digger

e. swimmer

(Here a student must understand the various bones and what their functions are. The student must then formulate a relationship between the type and formation of the bones and the activity that it would promote in a mammal.)

3. What would be the most logical result of mixing X and Y, both solubilized in distilled H_2O at room temperature?

a. precipitation of a solid

b. a change in color of the liquid

c. a rapid rise in temperature

d. a rapid decrease in temperature

(To answer correctly, a student must put together knowledge of X and Y as compounds with knowledge of their dissociations and the reactions of the individual components. All of the answers reflect outcomes that the student has previously experienced when two compounds are mixed.)

Evaluation Questions

1. Your fitness regimen involves jogging on the school track 2–3 miles per day with a friend. On a particular day, about 15 minutes into your jog, your friend suddenly pulls up and falls down, grasping her right calf in pain.

What should you do at that moment?
   a. apply ice to the calf
   b. apply heat to the calf
   c. tell her to get up and walk slowly
   d. get emergency help stat

(Here the student must be able to appraise the situation and evaluate the next course of action. The student's knowledge of both muscle function and injury are brought to bear in deciding which treatment to use.)

2. According to the American Heart Association, obesity plays a major role in early heart failure. Which of the below answers best describes how being severely overweight can cause the heart to falter?
   a. Obesity creates the need of greater blood volume in the circulatory system.
   b. Obesity creates the need for a quicker heart rate each minute.
   c. Obesity creates the need for a larger volume of blood exiting the heart per beat.
   d. Obesity causes the heart to grow larger than is anatomically recommended.
   e. Obesity causes the heart to develop a greater cardiac vessel network.

3. Abiotic factors impact heavily on photosynthetic richness in a green plant. The basic factors that influence sugar making in plants are (1) quantity of water, (2) quantity of sunlight, (3) quantity of CO_2, (4) environmental temperature, (5) movements of the air, and (6) richness of growth substrate. By moderately increasing in quantity, which of the factors would positively influence photosynthesis and which factors would negatively influence photosynthesis?
   a. + (1), (2), (3) and − (4), (5), (6)
   b. + (2), (3), (5), (6) and − (1), (4)
   c. + (1), (2), (3), (4), (5) and − (6)
   d. + (3), (4) and − (1), (2), (5), (6)
   e. + (1), (2), (3), (4) and − (5), (6)

Conclusion

Multiple-choice questions may be used effectively to assess student learning as long as they are constructed properly and include assessment of higher-order thinking. Taking the time to construct good stems and good answers, not only on the exams but also in the daily questions posed during the lesson, is well worth the effort. Practicing coming up with conclusions for critical-thinking questions is as important in creating high-level thinking in students as designing good-quality multiple-choice exams. Asking only non-challenging thinking questions during class is a waste of both the instructor's and students' time and does little to help assess student learning.

Reference

Bloom, B., M. Englehart, E. Furst, W. Hill, and D. Krathwohl. 1956. *Taxonomy of educational objectives: The classification of educational goals.* New York: McKay Publishers.

Chapter 6

Tips on Classroom Assessment: How to Teach Our Students to Take Multiple-Choice Exams

Linda Tichenor
Department of Biology
University of Arkansas
Fort Smith, Arkansas

While multiple-choice exams may not be the best way to assess students, they are one of the few assessment strategies available for large-lecture sections of students. I have been teaching several sections of anatomy and physiology with more than 90 students every semester for about six years and require a manageable method of assigning grades. I have found that administering five to six 50-question multiple-choice exams (100 points each) works best for me in terms of time allotted to grading. Part of my teaching practice utilizes case studies as a method of assessing writing and thinking skills; however, grading these is time consuming. Therefore, I might only assign two of them (100 points each) per semester. The four laboratory examinations measure skill in identification of structures (100 points each). The reality is that many students will continue into health care schools that also utilize multiple-choice questions for summative assessment. Board examinations even require high-level test-taking skills on multiple-choice tests.

Since I teach students who are recently out of high school or are returning after a hiatus in their learning experience, I realize that they need to be "taught" certain skills for taking multiple-choice examinations. They often have poor skills in reading and interpreting questions designed to assess at levels higher than Bloom's knowledge level.

As one solution for improving test-taking skills, I devised a strategy to focus on test errors. I would like to describe what I call the "One-Two-Three Test," which is a student self-analysis of performance. As a teaching practice, I always return lecture examinations quickly. I also return examinations in the smaller laboratory sections in order to give optimal chance of discussion and feedback.

When I return the examination, I ask the students to review it carefully and circle the correct answers on questions that they have missed. Then I ask them to reread each of these questions and categorize the type of error that they made in answering the question. Over the years, I have realized that students usually make errors for one of three reasons, which I lump into three "error categories."

The Type 1 Error is what I call a "head-banger." That is, when students see the correct answer on the test, they want to hit themselves in the head for being so careless. (They think this is very humorous and allows them to laugh at "dumb" mistakes.) These types of errors are usually followed by statements like, "I can't believe I put A on the Scantron form when I circled B on the test form!" "I don't know why I marked C when I knew that the answer was D!" "I don't know why I didn't mark the Scantron form when I clearly have the correct answer circled on the examination." This type of error also can be followed by, "I knew the answer, but I changed it at the last minute."

The Type 2 Error is what I have named "Something About the Question." This category error is followed by a statement like, "I understood the concept of the question, but something about the way the question was worded confused me." The Type 2 Error is sometimes described by the students as a "trick question." Usually when I am trying to create a higher-level multiple-choice question, the result is not fully understood by the student who may have superficial study skills or who may have memorized notes.

The Type 3 Error is the category described as, "I just didn't know the answer." In other words, the student did not study that particular concept

well enough, was not in class the day the material was covered, is not reading the textbook, or just did not pay enough attention in class to understand the concepts.

After the students have categorized all of their incorrect responses, I have them make a table on the front of their exam summing up the total questions missed in each category. This allows the students to see where they need to place emphasis on their next examination. I find this particularly instructive for students who make Type 1 Errors. Usually, it is a matter of instructing the students to slow down when reading and responding to the test item. If the Type 3 Errors are most numerous, this tells the student to spend more time in the classroom and to review more on a daily basis rather than cramming for the test the night before. The Type 2 errors are more informative for me as I learn how to construct really meaningful test questions. By using the test item analysis for many semesters, I have had insights into differences between students' use of language and mine (advanced learner). Even words such as "rigid" may not be in the students' lexicon although most faculty would be surprised that it is not.

Overall, taking the time to instruct students how to become better test-takers has improved both student performance and my test-making ability. I would highly recommend this technique for any instructor who has the disadvantage of teaching large lecture sections. Instructors may be surprised how much misunderstanding there can be in language differences between student and faculty!

Chapter 7

Better Multiple-Choice Assessments

William J. Straits and Susan Gomez-Zwiep
Department of Science Education
California State University, Long Beach
Long Beach, CA

Multiple-choice questions get a bum wrap; there's a multitude of reasons for including them in our assessment tool kits, yet the limitations of multiple-choice questions get much more press than the advantages. Foremost among their benefits, multiple-choice questions are fast. They can provide teachers and learners alike with immediate feedback about learning. Immediate feedback is of paramount importance, as it allows teachers and students to identify when they're progressing along the correct path and perhaps even more important, when they're straying off course (NRC 1998). Early recognition of how students are interpreting the content is key to effective and efficient learning and can help to amend misconceptions and even prevent their formation. Additionally, multiple-choice questions are easy to administer and score. Subsequently, multiple-choice assessments are often a preferred means for gaining information about student learning in large enrollment courses. Certainly, other forms of assessment (e.g., essay prompts and performance tasks) may provide deeper insight to student learning, but when multiple-choice questions are designed correctly, this disparity can be drastically reduced. This chapter is devoted to helping readers get the most out of their multiple-choice items.

Distracters

Typical multiple-choice questions include a prompt followed by several possible responses from which students must select the correct one. The incorrect options are called distracters, and these are a great and often untapped source of information for instructors… *if* they are designed to be informative. Multiple-choice questions can be constructed in ways that provide valuable information about student learning by using distracters that indicate specific misconceptions or gaps in understanding of the content. In other words, multiple-choice questions should contain one correct answer and two or three choices that match specific student errors or misunderstandings of the concept (Figure 1, adapted from Hardy et al. 2006).

When a student chooses an incorrect answer, the response provides information about that student's comprehension. Of course, creating these types of distracters requires a sophisticated understanding of student thinking about the concepts being tested. To be beneficial to instructors, distracters should be options that students might offer if they don't fully understand the material. How do you know what these "wrong" temptations are? There are several sources for information on typical student science misconceptions. (AAAS 1993; Keeley, Erberle, and Farrin 2005, 2007; Keeley, Erberle, and Dorsey 2008; Stephans 1994). However, the best source of plausible distracters may be your current students.

Distracters can be selected from student responses from pretests or quizzes given midway through your instruction. To use student work to generate distracters, first give the item as a "fill- in-the-blank" or "open-ended" question. Use the same or similar question prompt that you would with multiple-choice, but allow students to create their own answer (for example, "One indication of a chemical reaction is _____)." As you analyze students' answers, you will likely find several incorrect responses—all plausible—that can be used as distracters for the multiple-choice version on the same question on subsequent assessments. An additional benefit of this type of analysis is that in looking for incorrect answers you will notice common misconceptions among your students that can be addressed during instruction.

Adaptations

There are many variations to the standard multiple-choice format. In science, enhanced multiple-choice questions are often utilized as they allow one to assess both content and process items. In an enhanced multiple-choice question students are required to interpret tables, graphs, or some other type of diagram as part of the question. For example, the question may provide a graph within the prompt that students must interpret to select the correct response. Another possibility places the graphs as answer choices: Provide a prompt with various graphs as answer choices. This en-

FIGURE 1. Example problem: correct answer and potenial distractors

Given the volume of the cube that represents 16g of water, which cube(s) will sink in water? Circle the correct answer(s).

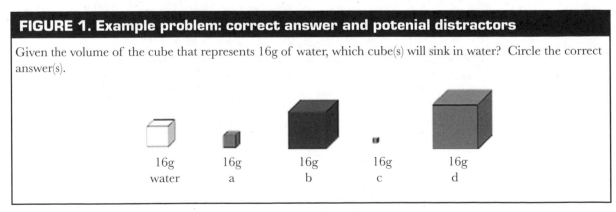

hanced multiple-choice format has the distinction of assessing the content taught and the skills of "doing" science simultaneously.

Another adaptation of a multiple-choice question is the justified multiple-choice item. In this format a typical multiple-choice item is given along with space for students to provide a written justification of their answer. For example, a multiple-choice question may be followed by a prompt such as, "answer ___ is the best answer because _____." This format provides you information beyond correct and incorrect choices, allowing you to identify students who answered incorrectly but understood the content to some extent and students who answered correctly, but for incorrect reasons. Scoring these items is eased by the use of rubrics, which provide a quick and easy method for scoring these items. The generic rubric shown below (Figure 2) can serve as a starting point as you develop rubrics for the specific questions included in your assessments. Use of this type of rubric speeds the scoring of justified multiple-choice questions while still providing richer information about students' learning.

Field-Testing

Did you assess the learning in the same way you taught it? Asking students to apply their knowledge to novel situations is a great way to see how deeply they have learned the information. However, there is a fine line between application of knowledge and confusion. If the situa-

tion is too novel, the students may not connect it to the content discussed in class. There is no way to know for certain how students may interpret a question until you have evidence (i.e., student work). This issued can be resolved by field-testing potential test items. This can be accomplished by mixing into your assessments a few untested questions that do not contribute to students' scores. Field-testing allows you to determine if students are able to interpret the question correctly or if the question needs revising. You can also randomly insert variations of the same question into different versions of the tests to see which wording/scenario performed the best.

Conclusion

Quality assessments provide a medium between your curriculum goals and student learning. However too often students fail our assessments, not because they don't know the material, but they don't understand what we are asking them about it. The key is to make sure that the assessments are valid and useful for our intended purpose: to assess what our students know in order to make our instruction purposeful and effective. Multiple-choice questions have an important place in the assessment of student learning and constructed correctly, can provide instructors and students alike with valuable insight to student learning.

FIGURE 2. Generic justified multiple-choice scoring guide

1	2	3	4
Incorrect answer and incorrect justification	Incorrect answer, and justification demonstrates an incomplete understanding. Or correct answer, and justification lacks logic	Correct answer, but justification is incomplete	Correct answer and complete justification. Shows understanding of concepts.

Section

2

References

American Association for the Advancement of Science (AAAS). 1993. *Benchmarks for science literacy*. New York: Oxford University Press.

Hardy, I., A. Jonen, K. Möller, and E. Stern. 2006. Effects of instructional support in constructivist learning environments for elementary school students' understanding of "floating and sinking." *Journal of Educational Psychology* 98: 307–326.

Keeley, P., F. Eberle, and L. Farrin. 2005. *Uncovering student ideas in science, vol. 1: 25 formative assessment probes*. Arlington, VA: NSTA Press.

Keeley, P., Eberle, F. & Farrin, L. 2007. *Uncovering student ideas in science, vol. 2: 25 MORE formative assessment probes*. Arlington, VA: NSTA Press.

Keeley, P., Eberle, F. & Dorsey, C. 2008. *Uncovering student ideas in science, vol. 3: Another 25 formative assessment probes*. Arlington, VA: NSTA Press.

National Research Council (NRC). 1998. Assessment in science education. In *National science education standards*. Washington DC: National Academy Press.

Stephans, J. 1994. *Targeting students' misconceptions: Physical science activities using the conceptual change model*. Riverview, FL: Idea Factory.

Chapter 8

Alternative Forms of Assessment for the College Science Laboratory

Kerry L. Cheesman
Capital University
Columbus, Ohio

Introduction

A significant part of the science education reform debate has involved assessment. Arguments continue to be made for and against various forms of assessment, and the terminology of assessment can be very confusing and frustrating. Traditional forms of assessment have usually included standardized or individualized tests such as multiple choice, true/false, and fill-in-the-blank. A basic definition of alternative assessment is any type of evaluation that does not use traditional forms of paper-and-pencil testing.

Contemporary science teaching stresses the need for students to be involved in their own learning in a hands-on, minds-on way, where learners construct their understanding from direct experiences with science concepts whenever possible. As a result, many science teachers have begun to embrace inquiry teaching in the classroom and in the laboratory. However, the breakdown in many attempts at reforming science teaching often comes down to assessment, because the assessment used for determining learning does not parallel the type of instruction employed in the classroom. Alternatively, the assessment (regional and national standardized exams in particular) drives the type of instruction rather than the other way around. Too often new forms of teaching and learning are coupled with traditional forms of student assessment rather than with forms that fit with the new ways of teaching.

Therein lies the rationale for using alternative forms of assessment in the undergraduate science laboratory. Many of the science education reform documents, such as the National Science Education Standards, call for students to gain a deeper understanding of science content through inquiry. Through inquiry laboratory experiences, questions are raised and answers are suggested based on multiple experiences surrounding specific content. This process models what practicing scientists do in their research toward discovering answers to their questions. Assessment of inquiry laboratory experiences must match the experience itself.

Assessment must begin with a firm understanding of what we want students to know and why we want them to know it. Is the goal of a laboratory session to have students memorize lots of organisms, reactions, or specimens? Or is it to give students the transferable tools needed for success in later courses and in their life journeys? These are two very different outcomes, and assessment of student learning must fit the intended outcomes.

Another question we must ask is "Why do we have labs?" We must answer this question before we can look at assessment of laboratory experiences. Is lab an extension of the classroom experience, or is it stand-alone? Does it presuppose knowledge and experience from the classroom, or does it begin with a relatively blank slate? Will assessment of the laboratory experience be tied to assessment of the classroom experience, or will it stand separately from it? Note here that the use of the term *laboratory* throughout this chapter implies all forms of hands-on science experiences. Labs can be traditional indoor experiences in any area of science but can also include field exercises, clinical experiences, computer/internet exercises, or any other venue that is designed to allow students a hands-on exposure to the principles and practices of science.

Bloom's Taxonomy

Before we begin looking at various forms of assessment, it is important to understand the various levels of cognitive evaluations that we can approach with our laboratory assessment tools. Bloom et al. (1956) described six levels of questioning that most college faculty are at least peripherally familiar with. The levels are

1. **Knowledge:** the ability to remember/recall previously learned material.
   Sample learning objectives in science: know common terms, know specific facts, know basic procedures and methods

2. **Comprehension (understanding):** the ability to grasp the meaning of material, and to explain or restate ideas.
   Sample learning objectives in science: understand facts and principles, interpret charts and graphs, demonstrate laboratory methods and procedures

3. **Application:** the ability to use learned material in new situations.
   Sample learning objectives in science: apply concepts and principles to new situations, apply theories to practical situations, construct graphs and charts

4. **Analysis:** the ability to separate material into component parts and show relationships between the parts.
   Sample learning objectives in science: distinguish between facts and inferences; evaluate the relevancy of data, recognize unstated assumptions

5. **Synthesis:** the ability to put together separate ideas to form a new whole or establish new relationships.
   Sample learning objectives in science: propose a plan for an experiment, formulate a new scheme for classifying, integrate multiple areas of learning into a plan to solve a problem

6. Evaluation: the ability to judge the worth or value of material against stated criteria.
Sample learning objective in science: judge the way that conclusions are supported by the data

The higher orders of Bloom's taxonomy require a different set of cognitive demands than do those at the lower end. If one is teaching using inquiry methods, assessment that uses higher-order questioning (application, analysis, synthesis, and evaluation) fits the teaching style and desired outcomes much better than do those questions which are at the lower level (knowledge and comprehension). Therefore, it is imperative that lab instructors know and use assessments that push students into higher-order thinking, rather than assessments that primarily address lower-order thinking.

Types of Assessment

So where are we as lab instructors on the assessment continuum? We can easily figure that out by looking at the four most common forms of undergraduate science lab assessment. They are

- *Weekly quizzes* covering last week's material or this week's reading, sometimes including turning in a flow chart of the current lab experiment.
- *Lab exams,* usually once or twice per semester, covering concepts and ideas learned in lab to date. These are often multiple-choice format, and ask students to identify such things as anatomy parts, organisms, appropriate reactions, or minerals.
- *Lab reports,* turned in weekly or less often. In most cases these are graded for the right answer and the right methods (a checklist of right things), and are often slanted toward finding or obtaining the right answer.
- *Solving an unknown* using methods taught in lab, with an expectation that the student will find

the right answer. This project is often weighted heavily in the lab or course grade, based on the false assumption that this really shows what a student knows.

Let's look at each of these assessment practices to determine what they really assess.

- *Weekly quizzes* are usually multiple-choice and/or fill-in format, with a high probability of simply being regurgitation of what is in the lab manual or the topic lectured on by the lab instructor. Assessment of student understanding is minimal at best and is often frustrating to students who do not do well with simple recall (memorization) questions.
- Most *lab exams* involve regurgitation as well (e.g., naming the same thing seen in the lab previously). They may be multiple-choice or fill-in formats; a few questions may be higher order, but most often they are simply recall level. Assessment of understanding is fairly minimal.
- *Lab reports,* if they are graded only for the right answer(s), are a poor assessment tool. If, on the other hand, one assesses the student's choices and techniques in arriving at the answer, lab reports can be good tools to determine student understanding (as well as misconceptions and errors in logic).
- *Solving an unknown* has the best probability of involving higher-order thinking, but it depends on the design of the problem. If it is completely open-ended, there is a better likelihood of being higher order. But what is really being assessed? If only the right or wrong answer is assessed, then this is not very useful. If, on the other hand, one assesses the logic and methodology used to obtain the answer, then one can get a good handle on student understanding and misconceptions.

If the assessment tool indeed assesses what we want to assess, then it is good. If not, how can we assess student laboratory experiences in a meaningful way, especially if we are looking at higher-order thinking in the labs themselves? How can we demonstrate to students that we are truly assessing their understanding rather than simply their ability to memorize?

Alternative Methods of Assessment

There are many ways to assess student understanding in the lab, besides the traditional methods listed above. Each has its own times and places where it works the best. Here are a few that have been shown to work in undergraduate science labs. For each, the level(s) of Bloom's taxonomy that the form of assessment is using is listed, along with the advantages and disadvantages of the method. Finally, a few examples of their use in undergraduate courses are noted.

1. ***Design/Build/Produce:*** In this synthesis-level assessment format each student is given a set of parameters to work with and is asked to design/build/produce a unique end product. The product uses knowledge previously gained in the lab or classroom, yet is new to the students involved.
   Advantages: Step-by-step thought processes can be assessed to see how students make connections, and where there are misconceptions.
   Disadvantages: This process takes time—it is often done outside of the allotted lab time; this always raises the question of copying from others (one solution is to assign the projects to groups instead of to individuals).
   Examples: Design a unique animal; demonstrate knowledge of physiological and biochemical concepts (zoology). Design a novel synthesis to get from material X to product Y (organic chemistry). Produce an equation that will allow the computer to model X (introductory computer science).

2. ***Classify:*** This is an application-level assessment. Students are asked to classify items not seen or worked with previously, using knowledge received in the lab or classroom. The process of classification is left up to the student.
   Advantages: This can be very helpful to diagnose misconceptions about various classification groups. Often there are plenty of items to classify, so each lab section can have its own set (less worry about sharing answers).
   Disadvantages: Instructors must be careful that exceptions to the rule (there are plenty in every field) do not discourage students who otherwise understand the material and the methods for classification.
   Examples: Determine the classification of animals not previously studied; demonstrate the ability to use classification keys (zoology). Classify minerals not previously studied; use keys and demonstrate an ability to use them (geology). Classify leaves or fruits not previously seen (botany).

3. ***Show/Demonstrate:*** Here the student physically demonstrates the correct use of a piece of equipment or a laboratory procedure within established parameters. This is comprehension level assessment.
   Advantages: The instructor can observe the student step by step and find misunderstandings easily; this is a very useful technique in skills-based or technical labs, but can also be very important in all fields of science.
   Disadvantages: This method requires one-on-one time with the instructor or other assessor, and in some cases space in the appropriate place.
   Examples: Demonstrate the correct preparation and use of a wet mount slide (general biology). Demonstrate correct glassware assembly for evaporation of a liquid (general chemistry). Show how to correctly streak a plate without contamination (microbiology).

4. ***Create a Poster:*** This technique may be at the comprehension, application, analysis, syn-

thesis, or evaluation level. The student designs a teaching poster on a given topic, and presents it to the instructor and/or the entire class. Students are expected to dig deep and show clearly what they have learned, and must be able to field questions from both classmates and instructors.

Advantages: A student must show understanding of the material in both written and oral formats. Since most students are strong in one or the other, a balance is achieved that allows students to have a chance to show what they really know.

Disadvantages: This is a time-intensive process; it can be very expensive if actually printing full-size posters (as opposed to printing mini versions or projecting the poster on a screen).

Examples: Research and present a mammalian disease, including its biological basis and treatment (biochemistry or immunology). Research and present an industrial process for a chemical application in industry (organic chemistry or environmental chemistry). Present the results of a field survey of soils, stratigraphy, or rock types (geology).

5. ***Explain the Data—Oral or Written:*** This assessment is at the application or analysis level, and is designed to help students think more deeply about a process or experiment they are involved in. A student must explain the details to the instructor, the class, or another group.

Advantages: This often involves charting or measurements, which can also be directly assessed; misconceptions are easily picked up.

Disadvantages: A student with poor writing or speaking skills may have understanding that is not adequately expressed to others.

Examples: After observing and measuring a closed ecosystem flask over time, explain what is happening to each species present (general biology). After observing and measuring a field site, explain what is happening there (must explain clues used to formulate answers)

(field biology/ecology/geology). After observing a demonstration (perhaps a clock experiment), explain what is happening in the flask (general chemistry).

6. ***Explain to a Child (or a Nonscience Major):*** The idea here is to shed the fancy terms and get to real understanding. A student must be able to formulate an explanation that relies only on basic vocabulary and examples. The explanation can be to a child or to a nonscience major at the college.

Advantages: Specific terminology (and misunderstanding of terms) doesn't get in the way of demonstrating true understanding of the subject.

Disadvantages: It may be hard for some students to explain concepts without using higher vocabulary, leading to frustration.

Examples: Explain to your 10-year-old sister why she looks quite different from you even though you both have the same parents (genetics). Explain what pH is and the difference in pH between coffee and baking soda (general chemistry). Explain what metamorphic rocks are and how they are formed (geology).

7. ***Become an Expert—Teach Others in the Class:*** "The best way to learn a concept is to teach it" is the framework for this assessment method, which can involve application, analysis, synthesis, or evaluation. Students are assigned (or choose from a list) topics to research and present; much like in a poster presentation, students must field questions from both their peers and from faculty, and are assessed on their ability to explain the connections and the concepts.

Advantages: Students really have to understand the material well, and must be able to relate it to other concepts previously studied or presented; peer pressure usually drives students to do well in front of the class.

Disadvantages: This method works best in the field or on a trip.

Examples: Become the expert on one or

two species that are expected to be seen on the field trip; when the species is encountered (or signs of it are), tell the group the essentials about the species and how it relates to others already encountered (ecology, zoology). Become the expert on one type of rock expected to be encountered in the field; when the rock is encountered, tell the group the essentials about it and how it relates to others already encountered (geology). Become an expert on one species of tree found on campus and teach others about it (botany).

8. ***Use Multiple-Choice Tests Using Higher-Order Questions:*** Using higher-order multiple-choice questions (Bloom's taxonomy) instead of lower-level ones increases critical-thinking skills and helps instructors understand not only what is and is not known, but also where misconceptions may be happening.
   Advantages: This technique assesses understanding of concepts instead of just recall of material as so many lab quizzes and exams do; grading can be fast and easy.
   Disadvantages: Some expertise is required to create good multiple-choice questions, especially at the synthesis and evaluation levels.

9. ***Use Group Assessments:*** Science in the workplace is almost always done in teams, often consisting of professionals with varied backgrounds and experiences. This can be mimicked in the lab by having experiments performed by groups. One can assess the performance and understanding of the group as a whole, thus requiring all members of the group to learn and contribute more to the overall effort (including teaching others within the group).
   Advantages: Knowing that they will be assessed as a group encourages all members to be involved in the project and to be equal partners; no one wants to be the weakest link.
   Disadvantages: Assessing all students in the group equally may not be realistic; this can often be overcome by allowing the group mem-

bers themselves to assess one another's participation in the group (this becomes a part of the overall assessment but does not take the place of the instructor's assessment).
   Examples: Students bring varied backgrounds such as history, music, and philosophy to the course; each one brings his or her unique perspectives, opinions, and abilities to bear in designing and carrying out the lab project (general education science courses).

Conclusion

As educators our goal should be increasing both the knowledge and understanding of our students. If we are teaching for better understanding, then we also need to be assessing understanding, rather than just knowledge (memorization). Real or enduring understanding goes beyond discrete facts or skills to focus on larger concepts, principles, and processes. Enduring understanding is applicable to new situations within or beyond the subject. Assessment of real understanding requires creativity on the part of the instructor. Authentic assessment needs to parallel the efforts of teaching, so that we discover not just what a student knows but what he/she truly understands. By using new and different forms of assessment, our laboratory experiences can challenge students to grow in enduring understanding.

Reference

Bloom, B., M. Englehart, E. Furst, W. Hill, and D. Krathwohl. 1956. *Taxonomy of educational objectives: The classification of educational goals.* New York: McKay Publishers.

Chapter 9

Assessment of Students' Learning Through the Creation of Scientific Posters

Kerry L. Cheesman and Nancy J. Swails
Capital University
Columbus, Ohio

Assessment of student knowledge takes many forms. One assessment we have used successfully in upper-division biology courses (immunology, biochemistry, histology, endocrinology) is presentation of scientific posters. These posters, on topics chosen by the students in consultation with course faculty, take the place of a traditional final exam, although they can also be used as a separate assessment during the semester (Cheesman 2004).

For these final projects, students conduct in-depth research on an agreed-upon topic. Depending on the course and the students involved, research may involve actual data collection, library research, or computer modeling. The list of topics is usually generated by the faculty since the list is distributed early in the semester, before students have had the opportunity to learn much about the field of study. Even so, faculty are open to topics of interest brought by students, so long as the topics requested are of an equal level of importance for the class in which the poster is being presented.

The research for the poster may be done over a few weeks or the entire semester, and may be done by individuals or in pairs. (Working together helps model the real world of scientific research.) Students must first define the questions that need to be addressed on the topic, and they must consult with the faculty to be sure that appropriate questions are being asked (and that no important questions are being left out). The instructor will also review with the researchers the flow of material to be presented to the class, noting other topics for which connections might be helpful.

Posters are generated as oversize (36″ × 48″) PowerPoint slides and printed using a large format poster printer purchased a few years ago by the university (the department pays for printing of the posters, which would otherwise be a financial hardship for some students).

Most students, prior to taking these upper-division courses, have participated in a required Research Methods course, where construction of scientific posters is covered in detail. For those students for whom this is a first poster attempt, the instructor is available to guide them through the mechanics of preparing the slide. Information about size and style of type, use of color, textbox formation, and other features is given to all students both in writing and by example. A variety of research posters prepared by students and faculty for meeting presentations hang in the department hallways, and students are encouraged to review these as models (good and bad) of poster design.

Early in the process students are also given an assessment rubric that has been prepared and modified within the department over time (see Figure 1). Students are assessed on their ability to prepare quality posters (an important goal within the department), but more important, on the quality of the research done and the ability of the students to relate the research to other topics in the course. Students are also assessed on their ability to present their posters to peers and department faculty (this also ties to departmental goals for all graduates), including their ability to respond to questions.

Student posters are presented at the end of the semester, either within a group or as part of the campuswide symposium on undergraduate research (spring semester only). The campus community is invited to view the posters and interact with the student authors, who prepare their presentations as they would for a professional society meeting. Assessment of the posters and the presentations, using the rubric provided to the students, is done by three members of the department faculty (independently). Scores from the assessment rubric are added together to produce a final score, and copies of the completed rubrics are returned to the students to help them know where they did well and where they need to improve for the future. Scores reflect not only the construction and presentation of the posters, but also the ability of the students to relate to varied audiences of faculty, science majors, and non-science majors.

Although students are often initially reluctant to make a presentation in front of dozens or hundreds of students and faculty from across the campus, their response to this method of assessment has been extremely positive. Students have routinely noted in class evaluations that they learned more from the research and poster session than they would have by studying for a comprehensive exam. Many students, taking a second advanced course in the department, have asked whether the poster option is available in the new course as well. Additionally, students have noted two years after the course that they still remember everything they learned by preparing and presenting their poster. This is far better retention than that found with traditional examinations. Thus, this method of assessing student learning has been shown to be beneficial to students and to increase retention of knowledge.

Reference

Cheesman, K. L. 2004. *Posters as a form of final exam.* Society for College Science Teachers Best Practices Series.

FIGURE 1. Poster scoresheet and criteria

Layout	1	2	3
• The title is descriptive and located at the top of the poster so that it is visible 15 to 20 feet away. Names and affiliations of the author(s) follows the title.	☐	☐	☐
• The content of the poster starts with an introduction or background and ends with conclusions or discussion (these sections are critical because they may be the only sections read). If appropriate, there should also be an abstract.	☐	☐	☐
• The flow of information through the poster is obvious, and the material is organized into columns.	☐	☐	☐
• Each illustration is of high quality; a caption makes the take-home message clear.	☐	☐	☐
• The poster has been carefully proofread for correct spelling and grammar.	☐	☐	☐
• The background color, presence of artwork, font color and style all contribute to the poster rather than distract from readability.	☐	☐	☐
Content	**1**	**2**	**3**
• The introduction or background provides a clear basis for the investigation.	☐	☐	☐
• The methods section clearly explains how the investigation was done.	☐	☐	☐
• The results are presented in a fashion clearly understandable by the intended audience. Figures and tables are used appropriately to relay information.	☐	☐	☐
• Conclusions or discussion follows from both the results and from the original intent of the investigation.	☐	☐	☐
• There is creativity and originality in the investigation.	☐	☐	☐
Knowledge of Topic	**1**	**2**	**3**
• The presenter(s) is familiar and comfortable with the material in the poster.	☐	☐	☐
• The presenter(s) is enthusiastic about the topic.	☐	☐	☐
• The presenter(s) knows more about the topic than what is presented in the poster.	☐	☐	☐
• Ideas are expressed about where the research may go next.	☐	☐	☐
• The presenter(s) communicates effectively and handles questions well.	☐	☐	☐
Bonus Points—overall impression			
TOTAL (50 possible points)			

Scoring
3 = Meets or exceeds standard, well done; 2 = OK / good, perhaps minor deficiencies; 1 = Clearly deficient in this area

Chapter 10

Using Electronic Portfolios for Assessment in College Science Courses: Instructor Guidelines and Student Responses

Jerry A. Waldvogel
Department of Biological Sciences
Clemson University
Clemson, South Carolina

Introduction

The past two decades have witnessed a dramatic shift in how we teach science. Key publications such as *Science for All Americans* (Rutherford and Ahlgren 1990), *Benchmarks for Science Literacy* (AAAS 1993), the *National Science Education Standards* (NRC 1996), and *Bio 2010* (NRC 2003) have led a wave of curricular reform that promotes inquiry-based instruction as the gold standard of pedagogy. Co-incident with this shift to a more student-centered approach to teaching, science classrooms have become increasingly technology driven (Cuban 2001; Haertel and Means 2003). Nowadays teachers are regularly using multimedia presentation systems to deliver course content and having students do likewise to teach their peers. Some teachers employ web-based tutorials to help students explore relationships and processes in science, while others utilize interactive technologies such as "clicker" systems to engage their students in real-time classroom learning. And a growing number are having their students develop audio and video podcasts that provide commentary about the interface between science and society. Yet despite the strong technological direction that student-centered instruction has taken, to date there has been no comparable technological shift in the assessment methods used to evaluate these new teaching strategies. More often than not, teachers are still using traditional in-class paper-and-pencil examinations, term papers, and lab reports to gauge student content knowledge and conceptual understanding. Many authors (e.g., Lord 1994, 1999; Young et al. 2003; Herreid 2004; Waldvogel 2004a, 2004b, 2006; French and Russell 2006) have discussed the problems that can stem from mismatches between instructional and assessment methods, especially when inquiry-based teaching is involved.

Electronic portfolios (hereafter referred to as e-portfolios) represent one possible way to bring assessment into alignment with technology-based instruction. In this chapter I briefly describe what characterizes an e-portfolio and how it can be used for assessment in college-level science courses. I then provide some guidelines for instructors on how to help students develop e-portfolios, along with a simple grading rubric for evaluating them. Finally, I present data from student reflections and course evaluations that speak to how students value e-portfolios in their science courses. My experience suggests that e-portfolios are useful assessment tools in science courses because they let students organize their work in ways that provide connection across a semester, allow self-assessment through reflection about that work, and generate links among important ideas across disciplines in ways that traditional assessment methods do not.

What Is An e-Portfolio?

It is not within the scope of this chapter to provide a detailed review of the rapidly growing literature on e-portfolios. Those with a general interest in the topic are referred to Cambridge et al. (2001) and Jafari and Kaufman (2006) for recent discussions. In addition, there is a large amount of information about e-portfolios now available on the internet, including the National Coalition for Electronic Portfolio Research (*www.ncepr.org*) and many distance learning organizations.

The idea of creating portfolios for college coursework is not new. For decades, college faculty in the arts and humanities have required stu-

dents to assemble paper portfolios of their written work in literature or composition courses, or photographic catalogues from fine art, architecture, and design classes. While these collections provide a centralized and chronological sequence of a student's work, they are often cumbersome to handle and store, and frequently lack a reflective component where the student demonstrates how work is linked together. Within the last 10–15 years, however, the portfolio concept has spread to many other types of courses. It has also become increasingly electronic with a strong emphasis on self-reflection (Yancey 2001). Indeed, reflective self-assessment represents the core of any well-crafted e-portfolio because it is what shows a student's intellectual development through time (Jafari and Kaufman 2006). Reflection also allows students to demonstrate the context-specific importance of their work and the connections among those works (Cambridge et al. 2001).

E-portfolios are like traditional paper portfolios in that they represent a collection of work from a course or other experience. But due to the highly interactive nature of the electronic tools used to create them, e-portfolios allow students to demonstrate their understanding in dynamic and creative ways. In this sense e-portfolios serve an assessment role not unlike concept maps (Novak and Gowin 1984) because they provide a view into the mental constructs students have about their work. And it goes without saying that the web-based nature of e-portfolios is also inherently appealing to today's "wired" generation of students.

e-Portfolios at Clemson University

The faculty at Clemson University has been using e-portfolios for nearly a decade. Starting with the influence of Kathleen Yancey, Arthur Young, and others in the Communication and Writing Across the Curriculum community, e-portfolio use has spread to a wide range of courses and programs. I have used e-portfolios as a portion of graded coursework in six different science courses since 2004. These include two introductory biology courses, three elective courses from our science and technology in society (STS) general education series, and an honors colloquium seminar on nature and enlightenment. Course sizes have ranged from as small as 11 to as large as 57. The total number of students who created e-portfolios in all of these courses is 327, although 45 of those portfolios carried over from one term to the next as part of the two-semester introductory biology courses.

I initially gave students free reign to develop any type of web-based e-portfolio they desired, but soon found that more guidance was needed to channel their creativity and focus them properly. I subsequently started providing a several-page handout that describe the basic idea behind e-portfolios and giving students three options for how to represent their work. The first is to create a freestanding website housed at their personal space on a university computer server. This method gives the most flexibility in design but does require that students master the basics of using web browser composition software. The second option is to use a free commercial website to host the e-portfolio. This method is simple in that it requires only a "drop-and-drag" understanding of file manipulation but is more creatively limiting and requires the user to tolerate commercial advertising on their portfolio. The third approach is to use the e-portfolio function of Blackboard, our course management software system. This method is simple and has the advantage of university-sponsored technical support, but it rather severely limits the student's artistic creativity and website design options.

Another thing I quickly learned is that, like other course assignments, students will procrastinate as long as possible before doing their work. Even honors students are not immune to this problem. I therefore instituted periodic e-portfolio checks throughout the semester to ensure that students keep up with the development of their portfolios. This has significantly improved both the technical quality of the e-portfolios I receive as well as the quality of the reflections they contain.

Table 1 (p. 62) is a checklist of key characteristics that I expect my students to have in their e-portfolios. The list is divided into four broad categories of overall design, examples of work, reflections, and links. By highlighting these key features of an e-portfolio (many of which are standards for basic web design), students understand from the very beginning of the course what is expected and on what the evaluation of their portfolio will be based. Outlining these expectations also gives students who need technical training on how to manage their portfolios ample time to acquire that knowledge.

Assessing e-Portfolios

Table 2 (p. 63) is a simple rubric for grading e-portfolios based on the characteristics described in Table 1. The basic rule of thumb for assigning point values to each category is to ask three questions. First, does the e-portfolio demonstrate the large majority of items for a given category (e.g., overall design)? Second, are there any significant flaws with respect to these categories (e.g., consistent misspellings or poor choices of font sizes and colors)? Third, is there something especially creative or insightful about the way the student has dealt with the information in this category?

I score my e-porfolios on a 100-point scale, but this is of course entirely up to the instructor and the particular grading scheme being used in a course. As with most assessment methods, it is recommended that e-portfolios not be the only form of student evaluation used, and that the total value given to the e-portfolio should not exceed 50% of the final course grade so as to avoid overpenalizing students who are less adept at this form of communication.

Personally, I believe that reflection is the most important category because it is where the students demonstrate their content knowledge and conceptual understanding of the course material. I therefore think it should be

---

TABLE 1. Checklist of key characteristics required in a course e-portfolio

Overall Design

- Clear evidence of critical thinking in the assignments/discussions displayed
- Reliable file access and loading: ALL FILES MUST OPEN WITHIN THE PORTFOLIO ITSELF (i.e., no Word documents)
- Use of proper spelling and grammar throughout
- Good readability (proper font size, color schemes, general layout, etc.)
- Clear navigation scheme (ease of use, reliable links to portfolio components, etc.)
- Brief description of the course to provide context for your portfolio
- Brief description of you
- Indicator on home page of date that the portfolio was last updated

Examples of Your Work

- At least three examples of what you consider to be your best work in the course
- Examples can include any graded assignment from the course or commentary on course lectures and discussions
- Clear links from these examples to your reflections about them (or you can imbed the reflections within the examples if you'd rather do it that way)

Reflections

- A separate reflection for **every** example of coursework included in the portfolio
- Overall reflection on the course and its value to your education
- Overall reflection about the value of making a course-related portfolio
- Clear and functional links between individual reflections and the works they refer to

Links

- Must all be active and go to correct site or document
- A link to your e-mail contact information
- As needed, relevant sites from which you drew information for this class
- Brief statement about why each link is relevant to you and/or your portfolio
- Other sites of personal interest are okay, but don't get carried away with these

---

weighted more heavily than other categories in this rubric.

One potential problem that I have encountered while grading e-portfolios is how to deal with the individual student personalities that often emerge in the interactive electronic environment. Unlike a multiple-choice test or standardized lab report, there is no one correct way to put together a good e-portfolio. This is another reason why I have gravitated to the rubric described above, since it focuses more on what is missing from the portfolio rather than on how what is there has been presented. While elegance and clarity can be rewarded, allowance also needs to be made for students who demonstrate understanding and connectivity among ideas but choose to do so in a more straightforward fashion. In other words, it is the ideas and links between those ideas that make for a good e-portfolio, not necessarily the technical savvy with which they are presented.

TABLE 2. A simple rubric for e-portfolios based on the categories shown in Table 1

	Correct information present?	Major flaws?	Creativity?
Overall Design			
Examples of Work			
Reflections			
Links			

Effects on Student Learning

Figure 1 shows the results of a summary analysis of the overall e-portfolio reflections (see Table 1) from the 327 e-portfolios that I have received in my courses. For this analysis I reviewed the reflection statements and scored them into one of three qualitative categories (No Value, Some Value, or High Value) based on the student's primary perception of the assignment. For example, if a student said that the e-portfolio was just busy work or that he did not see how it would affect his education or future employment, I scored it as No Value. If the student said that the exercise helped her appreciate the large amount of work she had done over the semester or that it gave her better perspective on topics outside the course content, I scored that as High Value. All other intermediate responses were scored as Some Value. A total of six different courses taught between 2004 and 2007 are included in the analysis.

Approximately one-quarter of the students indicated that the e-portfolio assignment was of no significant value to them. In addition to categorizing it as busy work, many said that they did not see the value of cataloguing work that I had already seen and graded, or indicated that the amount of work needed to master the nec-

FIGURE 1.
Qualitative scoring of student views of e-portfolios

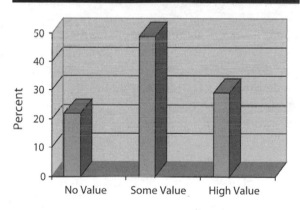

essary computer skills to make the portfolio was not worth the effort. On the other hand, almost three quarters of my students saw some or high value in the e-portfolio experience. Comments here ranged from pragmatic explanations about learning useful computer skills to descriptions of having acquired new perspectives on topics as a result of having to organize and reflect on their work. Of those who assigned some or a high degree of value to the e-portfolio assignment, virtually all of them said that after having gone through the process of creating an e-portfolio, they hoped it was something they would be able to do again in another course. While these are self-reported views and thus subject to bias, my personal sense is that the students were being genuine in their statements about the value of their e-portfolio experience.

An additional source of comments about these e-portfolios comes from anonymous online course evaluations. While these evaluations are far fewer in number (~55–60% of our students submit forms at the end of a semester), they perhaps have more credibility due to their anonymous nature. Of those students who made direct comments about the e-portfolio assignment in their evaluations, 68% (or approximately the same percentage as in the identified reflections) indicated that they viewed e-portfolios as having some or high value. I take this result to indicate a reasonably high degree of reliability between the two sources of student opinions.

Finally, several of the identified reflections and anonymous evaluations indicated that the main benefit of the e-portfolio assignment was that it forced students to think about the material covered in the course as an entire body of knowledge that is connected to a range of other scientific and social issues. One student summarized the experience well by saying,

> *The e-portfolio made me realize just how linked together science is with non-scientific issues. I don't think I've ever been given the chance in my other courses to see that kind of connection, and I kind of like it! This was a worthwhile experience.*

Conclusion

A growing body of literature now points to the successes (and potential drawbacks) of using e-portfolios as assessment tools in higher education (Jafari and Kaufman 2006). These studies come from multiple course types, a range of academic settings, and many diverse cultures, all of which speak to the broad applicability of this form of assessment. E-portfolios appeal to the technological interests of young people, allow for almost limitless ways of creative self-expression, and interface seamlessly with the technology already in use in the science classroom.

My own experience using e-portfolios for assessment in college-level science classes has been very positive. While there are indeed technological and course management obstacles that must be overcome when using this practice, the student-learning benefits that result appear to be real and in a direction consistent with the objectives of inquiry-based, constructivist teaching. As computer technologies continue to improve, the tools available for developing thoughtful and creative student e-portfolios will only be enhanced, and thus the online world stands to become a valuable and highly flexible tool for assessing student understanding in science. E-portfolios are therefore a welcome addition to the science classroom because they engage our students in the kind of intellectual connection building and self-reflection that is key to successful inquiry-based education.

Acknowledgments

I am most grateful for the patience and good humor of my students who have put up with much instructional "innovation" over the years in my courses. I thank them for their honesty in evaluating these classroom experiments. I also thank my Clemson faculty colleagues in the Writing and Communication Across the Curriculum programs, as well as the Teaching and Learning Creatively project, for their insight regarding novel ways of teaching. In particular Art Young, Patti Connor-Greene, Catherine Mobley, and Catherine Paul have given especially cogent advice. I have learned much of what I know about e-portfolios from Kathleen Yancey and Gail Ring; thanks to them for much wise council. Jeffrey Appling has been a steadfast administrative supporter of e-portfolios at Clemson University, and I hereby gratefully acknowledge his dedication to exploring new and interesting ways to assess student understanding. This work was supported in part by professional development funds provided by the Roy and Marnie Pearce Center for Communications at Clemson University.

References

American Association for the Advancement of Science (AAAS). 1993. *Benchmarks for science literacy*. New York: Oxford University Press.

Cambridge, B. L., S. Kahn, D. P. Tompkins, and K. B. Yancey. 2001. *Electronic portfolios: Emerging practices in student, faculty, and institutional learning*. Washington, DC: American Association for Higher Education.

Cuban, L. 2001. *Oversold and underused: Computers in the classroom*. Cambridge, MA: Harvard University Press.

French, D. P., and C. P. Russell. 2006. Converting laboratories from verification to inquiry. In *Handbook of college science teaching*, eds. W. Leonard, and J. Mintzes, 203–212. Arlington, VA: NSTA Press.

Haertel, G. D., and B. Means, eds. 2003. *Evaluating educational technology*. New York: Teachers College Press.

Herreid, C. F. 2004. Can case studies be used to teach critical thinking? *Journal of College Science Teaching* 33 (6): 12–14.

Jafari, A., and C. Kaufman. 2006. *Handbook of research on e-portfolios*. Hershey, PA: Idea Group Reference.

Lord, T. 1994. Using constructivism to enhance student learning in college biology. *Journal of Science Teaching* 23 (5): 346–348.

Lord, T. 1999. A comparison between traditional and constructivist teaching in environmental science. *The Journal of Environmental Education* 30 (3): 22–27.

National Research Council (NRC). 1996. *National science education standards*. Washington, DC: National Academy Press.

National Research Council (NRC). 2003. *Bio 2010: Transforming undergraduate education for future research biologists*. Washington, DC: National Academy Press.

Novak, J. D., and D. R. Gowin. 1984. *Learning how to learn*. London: Cambridge University Press.

Rutherford, F. J., and A. Ahlgren. 1990. *Science for all Americans*. New York: Oxford University Press.

Waldvogel, J. A. 2004a. Implications of future biological research for the biology curriculum. In *Biology and the physics-first curriculum: A symposium celebrating BSCS's 15th anniversary*, eds. R. Bybee, and A. Gardner, 15–19. Colorado Springs, CO: Biological Sciences Curriculum Study.

Waldvogel, J. A. 2004b. Writing poetry to assess creative and critical thinking in the sciences. In *Teaching tips: Innovations in undergraduate science instruction*, eds. M. Druger, E. D. Siebert, and L. M. Crow, 58–59. Arlington, VA: NSTA Press.

Waldvogel, J. A. 2006. Mating Darwin with Dickenson: How writing creative poetry in biology helps students think critically and build personal connections to course content. In *Handbook of college science teaching*, eds. J. L. Mintzes, and W. H. Leonard, 185–194. Arlington, VA: NSTA Press.

Yancey, K. B. 2001. Digitized student portfolios. In *Electronic portfolios: Emerging practices in student, faculty, and institutional learning*, ed. B. L. Cambridge, 15–30. Washington, DC: American Association for Higher Education.

Young, A., P. Connor-Greene, C. Paul, and J.
Waldvogel. 2003. Poetry across the curriculum:
Four disciplinary perspectives. *Language and
Learning Across the Disciplines* 6 (2): 14–44.

Chapter 11

Wetscience: A Means of Assessing Math, Science, and Technology Incorporation Into a Service Learning Outreach Program

Mark A. Gallo
Niagara University
Niagara University, NY

Introduction

The integration of math, science, and technology (MST) into robust inquiry-based learning opportunities is a tall order for any educator. However it is especially critical to do so throughout the learning process, most notably during middle school, when the subjects begin to be treated by the schools as separate, disconnected classes. The fundamental concepts for many subjects are learned at a young age. It is during this time that the basic content knowledge and skills that pave the way for further cognitive development and conceptual understanding are learned (Newton 1997).

All too often science has been treated as a historical study of known facts instead of a way of discovery; math has been treated as a walk through the disciplines of geometry, algebra, and trigonometry, and for those that "get it," an introduction to calculus; and technology is relegated to discussions about an amorphous something that somehow makes our lives easier, thanks to things like computers, remote controls, MP3 players, and microwave ovens. The goals of the disciplines become distorted as the outcomes and products are heralded, but not the processes themselves. Many teachers in schools have been forced to concentrate on what the students learn and not on how they learn it, as more standardized tests are used to assess the students. Skill competency is taking a back seat to content as teachers "teach to the test." Students begin to see the subjects as hard,

Chapter 11

Wetscience: A Means of Assessing Math, Science, and Technology Incorporation Into a Service Learning Outreach Program

Section 2

challenging, and not all that interesting or related to their level of understanding of the workings of the world around them. Although science education reforms have been introduced (NRC 1996; AAAS 1993) there still is a long way to go for universal adoption of these guidelines.

Yet there is another way. Experiential learning involves the learner in a meaningful project. An individual takes a greater interest in a project that has relevance to one's own life. The learning is always at the right level, as it is self-directed and self-motivated. This approach leads the student to become more self-reliant, self-regulating, and self-evaluating in completing the lessons. The technology is available as a learning resource, the scientific method is used as the method of inquiry, and the mathematics is the way to measure and assess the outcome. Hands-on, minds-on learning should be one of the most important goals, if not the most important goal, of MST education. It should be noted that the national science standards stress validation of material through experiential learning.

Another place where experiential learning is a valuable component of one's education is during preservice teacher training. Discipline-specific content and pedagogy are typically taught in two different departments, or perhaps even in different colleges in the educational arena. There is very little connection between the two; therefore students must make their own associations to link the concepts in a useful and meaningful way for their future profession. One way to assist these individuals is to enjoin them in situations where they can see master teachers in a classroom situation so that they may model their behavior. Creating a learning environment that applies inquiry is a challenge, especially if one is not used to this pedagogical stance. Therefore preservice teachers who participate in such an experience will understand the student's perspective, as they will be put into that role at times through the experience. Luft (2001) noted the impact that such an experience had on the teachers. Student placements sometime fall short in this respect in that the host

teacher may not be a good role model or may not create the appropriate environment for fruitful interaction. This study addresses some of these deficiencies through a university-school partnership for MST education.

Methods

Niagara University has a strong commitment to community service learning. It is a part of the mission of the University and the teachings of St. Vincent DePaul to assist those less fortunate with whatever means possible. In keeping with the mission of the institution, the author has been involved in service learning projects concerning science outreach with numerous schools. The common theme of water quality monitoring was used as a starting point to demonstrate the interrelationships among math, science, and technology. "Would you drink this water?" was one of the questions that students were asked to consider in a qualitative and quantitative manner. Common misconceptions about environmental health were explored, and in nearly every instance they were resolved. This was assessed through the student's answers on pre- and postvisit questionnaires. The classroom experience was made relevant in that in each situation the initial water sample was gathered from a location near the school. The Niagara region is also the site of Love Canal and a number of questionable environmental practices; therefore, it was a simple matter to begin a discussion regarding a topic about which everyone had some preconceived notions and opinions (many of which were based on falsehoods). Students were taught how to use a number of Vernier probes and then allowed to keep them at the school for their own analyses. Students at the schools became environmental stewards and continued to gather data on the properties of their adopted watershed. The students shared their data by placing it on a web server. Comparisons of the data allowed for further expansion of the initial topics. Individuals began to ask additional questions about environmental health, which has led to further investigations.

The activities stressed the impact of physical and chemical parameters on the biological world. Serial dilution was performed; therefore mathematics was a part of the exercise. The discussion moved from the concrete, "Does this tube look less turbid (cloudy) than the previous one?" to the abstract "How much could you dilute something and still need to be concerned about the presence of the material?" The water samples were typically small (several hundred milliliters), and so the biological world that was present in these samples was microscopic. It was decided to focus on the microbial world, and use it as a starting point to relate to all other living organisms. This is appropriate and reasonable, as many curricula discuss food webs or food pyramids and the microbes are the major players in every ecosystem. The microbial world is an unfamiliar one to most students and teachers. This study presented a particular opportunity to demonstrate to pre- and in-service teachers the valuable lessons that can be learned with the microbes and why lessons involving them should be incorporated into the standard curriculum.

Results

Nearly seven hundred students from surrounding middle schools have been involved in the school visitation program. The school visitation pre- and post-questionnaires produced some interesting findings (see Figures 1 and 2). The questionnaire below was provided to the teacher in advance of visitation by individuals from Niagara University. The K–12 students were told to take them home and work on them at their own pace. It was stressed that the questions were not an exam, and that the teacher would not use them toward the students' grades.

FIGURE 1. Pre- and postquestionnaire for grades 7 and 8

1. What is the next metric unit smaller than a centimeter?
2. How do you determine the magnification power of a compound light microscope?
3. A centimeter (cm) is about a half an inch. How many bacteria stretched end to end would fit in a cm?
4. How many bacteria stretched end to end would be the length of a cheek cell?
5. Can you see bacterial contamination of a clear liquidlike water? (Can you tell if water is safe to drink by looking at it?). Explain your answer.
6. Do you think you will find bacteria in every sample from a natural environment? Explain why or why not.
7. What do bacteria look like?
8. How can you differentiate bacteria from other types of living things?
9. How many different types of bacteria do you think there are?
10. In what kind of environments will you find high numbers of bacteria?
11. If you could observe soil using "super-microvision" what might you see the microbes in the soil doing?
12. Do bacteria carry out the same life functions as us? Explain.
13. What sorts of interactions may bacteria have with other organisms?
14. Are all bacteria harmful to us? Explain.
15. Where can you find bacteria on us?
16. Do you have any other questions about microbiology or bacteria?

Chapter 11

Wetscience: A Means of Assessing Math, Science, and Technology Incorporation Into a Service Learning Outreach Program

A scoring rubric was developed and students' answers were scored accordingly. Answers for a question such as "What do microbes do in the environment?" changed from typically "I don't know," or "They can make you sick," prior to visitation to "You may see them moving, looking for food, and multiplying"; "They may decompose materials found in their environment"; "They may be found nearly everywhere"; "They can live on us and some make you sick and others won't"; and "They may be present in water, even if you can't see them." The students arrived at many of these answers as a result of their own discovery.

FIGURE 2. Average score for questionnaire grades 7 and 8

Question	Pre	Post	Difference
1	2.60	2.73	0.13
2	1.30	2.19	0.89
3	0.78	1.90	1.12
4	0.65	1.83	1.18
5	1.61	2.69	1.08
6	1.96	2.82	0.86
7	1.16	2.18	1.02
8	0.71	1.62	0.91
9	1.87	2.53	0.66
10	1.84	2.70	0.86
11	1.43	2.68	1.25
12	1.00	2.10	1.10
13	0.94	2.06	1.12
14	1.55	2.73	1.18
15	2.06	2.81	0.75
16	N/A	N/A	N/A

Discussion

Certain reflective pieces by the preservice teachers indicated that this experience was "one of the best in my life," that "every teacher should go through this," and "wow, there is a lot preparation for labs."

Student misconceptions are a challenge to the educator. Incorrect beliefs are hard for the learner to reevaluate in an objective fashion, and it is therefore extremely important that when students are introduced to new topics, they are learning them correctly (Bybee 2002). If science is taught in a lecture format, then it is up to the learner to synthesize one's own interpretation of the lesson. A value to hands-on activities is the student can be led toward a path of self-discovery. This was true in that the students were given questionnaires prior to the experience and during the school visitations students were asked to make predictions on the outcomes of activities and justify their answers prior to experimentation. There was active discussion about alternative solutions, and the author would guide the discussion toward certain avenues. "Wrong" answers were used as a way to uncover underlying misunderstanding, and gaps were filled in so that the students could come up with their own ideas and eliminate others to arrive at an appropriate conclusion. Others have recognized the value of problem-based questions followed by open discussions (Peat, Taylor, and Fernandez 2002). The students used directed inquiry as a means to become more actively involved in their education, a mechanism that has shown to be effective by others (Newton 1997).

It is not enough for teahcers to merely point out the learners' incorrect assumptions but rather it is important to provide students with a way to arrive at a parsimonious state in light of new information. Learners must make new connections and possibly reorient their thinking about a particular subject. Failure to do so will typically cause students to fall back into former beliefs as soon as the test is over (AAAS 1993). One of the encouraging findings from this study was a general increase in average scores in every question. Some of the questions required extension beyond the content, and hence it appeared that the students were able to transfer their understanding to novel situations.

The classroom activities were well aligned with the New York State (2008) and national (NRC 1996) science standards. The activities were valuable elaborations for a number of reasons.

First, the expertise for many middle school teachers is not in the sciences and hence the teacher may shy away from particular topics. One of the goals was to alleviate the fears that teachers may have of incorporating technology in general and computers in particular into the classroom. All of the equipment was available to the teachers during the school year. This deficiency had been noted by others, especially as it relates to integration of technology into classroom activities (Stevens 1995). Royer (2002) noted that only 20% of teachers felt comfortable and confident with technology. One point that was stressed in this study was the impact and importance of the microbial world on the environment.

Second, there was hesitancy by the teacher to "add" anything to the tight curriculum. It was stressed that these experiences would replace traditional offerings. The Vernier probes were used to explore temperature, pH, conductivity, turbidity, and solubility of materials in water. Apple Powerbook computers were used in conjunction with the Vernier equipment to analyze the data. Such integration of technology enhanced student learning and made the technolgy's value purposeful. The technology was not an afterthought or an add-on, but rather it was necessary to derive a quantitative answer. Such use has been shown to be of merit (Dockstader 1999; Royer 2002). Technology integration can't happen if it is not available or appropriate. It was important that the tools were available for the students to pose their own questions or approach new areas of study with their larger tool sets; therefore, the investigator supplied each classroom with the probes for continued use. Motivated students continued

Chapter 11

Wetscience: A Means of Assessing Math, Science, and Technology Incorporation into a Service Learning Outreach Program

with this project as noted by water sample collection and uploading of their data onto the public server. The U.S. government has recognized the issues associated with poor technology integration and has spent more than $275 million on a program called "Preparing Tomorrow's Teachers to Use Technology (PT3) to assist preservice teachers. This project was in direct alliance with the directives of that program and has been instrumental in enlisting preservice teachers in a mentoring relationship to develop the experience necessary to feel comfortable incorporating technology into their curriculum in the future.

Third, the novelty of the approach of the investigator compared to the typical classroom activity was evident. A more conceptual approach was followed, and the familiarity of the material and the depth of understanding of the subject by the investigator appeared to be more engaging for the students. Beause the equipment worked, no time was necessary to "figure things out" and the students wer not afraid to try it, which is an important consideration (Salpeter 2002).

Fourth, the students were responsible for "the answers." There was no answer sheet and the outcome was not known ahead of time by the people in charge, so the burden of collecting the evidence fell squarely on the student. Wadsworth (1984) observed that children learn best when they can actively participate in the content they are trying to learn. They can complete their action and incorporate their new knowledge into their existing schema and use this knowledge in future experiences.

Fifth, the questions that were provided on the pre- and postsurveys, as well as those addressed during the visits to the schools, could not be answered with a yes or no. The questions required higher-order thinking skills, as outlined by Bloom (1989) and reiterated by Anderson and Sosniak (1994). There is a large body of information and discussion related to Bloom's work that he started in the 1950s. Synthesis and evaluation involve higher cognitive skills, and the types of analyses that the students were asked to perform take

this into consideration. Interestingly, both low- and high-performing students benefited from this experience, a phenomenon that had been discussed by others (Brewton, 2003). Therefore this experience was in keeping with the goals of NCLB legislation.

Sixth, everybody had some preconceived notion about the subject material. Simonneaux (2000) had surveyed fifth graders about microbes and found that they typically saw microbes as bad things and that other beliefs about the properties of microbes were also inaccurate. This author noted the same trend. However, it should be noted that the students were quick to challenge and correct their own misconceptions if allowed to investigate the phenomenon. The astute instructor is able to recognize the deficiencies and misconceptions and design activities to enhance, expand, and refine the learner's understanding. Proficiency in microscopy is something that all students should learn in middle school, but many schools lack the equipment and supplies to make it a positive experience. Also it is logistically challenging for the teacher to verify that each individual is acquiring a suitable image. The author was able to provide excellent imaging via the use of videomicroscopy; it was typically one of the highlights of the school visit. Shrieks of "yuck" or "cool" or "whoa" were the norm. The presence of active, interactive critters from all sorts of locations was enlightening to nearly all students. Videomicroscopy made the microbial world become a tangible, visible world. The students were primed to explore other locations for the presence of microbes after visualizing microorganisms.

The preexposure provided enough background knowledge to allow them to create their own hypotheses about the types of environments where one could find microbes. The very concrete example of visualization led to the very abstract activity of predicting the microscopic inhabitants in a location. The hunt for microbes was not an exercise in inquiry for its own sake. Rather it was useful in reaching the planned objectives related to defining the requirements, elements, organisms of an ecosystem. It was a productive question in that it engaged the learner in an exercise to take a closer look at a particular environment. The inquiry also went beyond the classroom, both literally and figuratively. Students were encouraged to use their own water samples. Water analysis was part of an awareness of their local water supply, but also allowed them to be the creators and owners of knowledge. Individuals could opt to continue to monitor an environment, and they were encouraged to do so. Their information was considered significant and valuable and they were provided with a website containing a way for them to add their findings to the database. The extended period of study reinforced the importance of the knowledge.

Microorganisms provide a nice area for study because of their importance, impact, and relevance to everyone's life. The power of the unseen world has not gone unrecognized by others. A four part-science documentary titled *Intimate Strangers: Unseen Life on Earth* had been produced by Baker and Simon Associates in conjunction with Oregon Public Broadcasting. A book that is a nice complement to the series, with the same title, was also produced (Needham et al. 2000). Though we tend to think of our interactions with them as minimal at best, microbes actually play a large role in our lives. They are typically thought of as disease-causing agents, and although that is true for a very small percentage of them, the potential danger is a grave concern, and always in the news, as disease has had a major impact on societies throughout the ages.

Many point to the Third International Mathematics and Science Study (TIMSS) results (NCES 2003) and ask why particular countries and school systems achieved a particular ranking. It has been noted that the American students do not rank very well on the eighth-grade test (Dove 2002). It appears that school systems that stress providing the information in a manner related to a practical problem showed higher test scores. Kiker (2007) recommended that we should continue to use existing standardized assessments for accountability and exit requirements, but should continue to develop and implement performance-based demonstrations of skills and knowledge that can give a better picture of a student's skills.

Another strategy that appeared to be effective was the use of brainstorming sessions to call on the learner's past experiences and knowledge (Moore and Huber 2001). Obviously it is the teacher's responsibility to direct these students toward questions that can be approached with the materials on hand. Mediation of the discussion is important, and it requires an instructor who is not only well versed in science, but able to explain important concepts and content in a relevant way. Professional development is becoming a big part of many school districts' policies (Smith and DeSimone 2003). This program is not unique. Anderson (2005) described a program whereby engineering students met with middle school students to design long-term projects. The EPICS program has grown beyond that institution and is carried out by a number of other institutions. Gutstein, Smith, and Manahan (2006) have established a Science Education Outreach Program that engages undergraduates in service-learning programs at area schools.

Postbaccalaureate institutions are beginning to rethink the goals of preparing their students for the future. Trautmann and Krasney (2006) describe the successes of placing science and engineering graduate students in the classroom. The National Science Foundation has established teaching fellowships (NSF 2005). An initial concern of faculty advisors was that the program would take the graduate students away from their primary goal of completing their scientific research. Studies of Cornell graduate students who were actively involved in Graduate–K12 science inquiry partnerships (CSIP) showned that most of their mentors were pleased with the attitudinal changes of the participants. They noted that some were more focused on their research and much better in posing questions and had dramatically improved presentation and teaching skills (Cornell 2008).

Chapter 11

Wetscience: A Means of Assessing Math, Science, and Technology Incorporation into a Service Learning Outreach Program

Acknowledgments

The author would like to thank the American Society for Microbiology and the Waksman Foundation for Microbiology for inspiration and support.

References

American Association for the Advancement of Science (AAAS). 1993. *Benchmarks for science literacy*. New York: Oxford University Press.

Anderson, L. W., and L. A. Sosniak. 1994. *Bloom's taxonomy: A forty-year retrospective.* Chicago, IL: National Society for the Study of Education.

Anderson, S. 2005. EPICS exploration. *Science Scope*. 28 (7): 28–29.

Bloom B. S., ed. 1989. *Taxonomy of educational objectives, handbook I: Cognitive domain.* New York: McKay.

Brewton, C. C. 2003. Science for all: Can "no child left behind" make a difference? *The Science Teacher* 70: 10.

Bybee, R. W. 2002. Biology education in the United States: The unfinished century. *Bioscience* 52: 560.

Cornell Science Inquiry Partnerships (CSIP). *http://csip.cornell.edu*

Dockstader, J. 1999. Teachers of the 21st century know: The what, why and how of technology integration. *THE Journal* 26: 73.

Dove, A. 2002. It takes a village to raise an idiot: Fixing U.S. science education. *The Journal of Clinical Investigation* 110: 1057.

Gutstein, J., M. Smith, and D. Manahan. 2006. A service-learning model for science education outreach. *Journal of College Science Teaching* 36:22–26.

Kiker, J. 2007. Move beyond seat time and narrowly defined knowledge and skills. *Techniques*. May: 38–41.

Luft, J. A. 2001. Changing inquiry practices and beliefs: The impact of an inquiry-based professional programme on beginning and experienced secondary science teachers. *International Journal of Science Education* 23: 517.

Moore, C. J., and R. A. Huber. 2001. Support for environmental education from the national science education standards and the internet. *The Journal of Environmental Education* 32: 21.

National Center for Education Statistics. (NCES). 2003. TIMSS Results. *Trends in international mathematics and science study*. Available online at *http://nces.ed.gov/timss/results03.asp*.

National Research Council (NRC). 1996. *National science education standards*. Washington, DC: National Academy Press.

National Science Foundation (NSF). 2005. *NSF graduate teaching fellows in K–12 education (GK-12) program solicitation* (NSF 05-553). Arlington, VA: National Science Foundation.

Needham, C., M. Hoagland, K. McPherson, and B. Dodson. 2000. *Intimate strangers: Unseen life on Earth*. Washington, DC: ASM Press.

Newton, L. R. 1997. Information technology in biological teaching: Challenges and opportunities. *Journal of Biological Education* 31: 274.

New York State Education Department. 2008. Science learning standards and core curriculum. Available online at *www.emsc.nysed.gov/ciai/mst/scirg.html*.

Peat, M., C. Taylor, and A. Fernandez. 2002. From information technology in biology teaching to inspiration technology: Where have we come from and where are we going? *Australian Science Teachers' Journal* 48: 6.

Royer, R. 2002. Supporting technology integration through action research. *Clearing House* 75: 233.

Salpeter, J. 2002. Training teachers. *Technology & Learning* 22: 52.

Simonneaux, L. 2000. A study of pupils' conceptions and reasoning in connection with "microbes," as a contribution to research in biotechnology education. *International Journal of Science Education* 22: 619.

Smith, T. M., and L. M. DeSimone. 2003. Do changes in patterns of participation in teacher's professional development reflect the goals of standards-based reform? *Educational Horizons.* 81: 119.

Stevens, J. E. 1995. The growing reality of virtual reality. *Bioscience* 45: 435.

Trautmann, N. M., and M. E. Krasny. 2006. Integrating teaching and research: A new model for graduate education? *Bioscience* 56:159–165.

U.S. Department of Education. 2008. *No child left behind information page.* Available online at *www.ed.gov/nclb/landing.jhtml.*

U.S. Department of Education. 2008. *Preparing tomorrow's teachers to use technology program (PT3).* Available online at *www.ed.gov/ programs/teachtech/index.html.*

Wadsworth, B. J. 1984. *Piaget's theory of cognitive and affective development* (3rd Edition). New York: Longman Publishing.

Chapter 12

Gauging the Nature of Science (NOS): An Alternate Form of Assessment

Thomas J. Melvin
Biology Department
Indiana University of Pennsylvania
Indiana, Pennsylvania

The biggest gap that adults have in their scientific knowledge is not that they've forgotten the details of DNA; it's rather that they don't know what science is about. Understanding the nature of science is even more important than mastering its details.
—Alan Leshner, AAAS
Educational Leadership,
December 2006

When a teacher wishes to assess a student's performance, he or she often gives an exam or quiz that is usually based on lecture notes or reading assignments. Most students can perform well by simply memorizing the relative material without fully understanding the concepts. As educators, it is our duty to instill a higher level of learning that cannot be achieved through the memorization and regurgitation of facts. Higher-level learning ultimately stems from the teaching strategy of the instructor. Current studies show classrooms taught through inquiry often demonstrate higher course grades when compared to classrooms taught in a more traditional manner (Anastasiow et al. 1970; Travis and Lord 2004). Bell, Binns, and Smetana (2005) define inquiry teaching as a form of instruction in which students take an active role in learning and teachers emphasize questions, data analysis, and critical thinking. More important, inquiry instruction may better convey basic scientific processes as students discover the foundations of science through critical thinking and investigative laboratories.

Many students can pass science courses in high school and college and still not be able to set up a properly controlled experiment. Although they may have performed relatively well in science courses, their understanding of scientific processes are relatively low. Science teachers of all disciplines can use students' NOS (nature of science) scores as an alternate form of assessment. In addition to traditional forms of assessment like exams and quizzes, NOS levels can truly indicate a class's understanding of scientific processes. Higher-level learning in science classrooms can usually be correlated with a more thorough understanding of the nature of science (Lederman et al. 2002).

Historically, there has been a debate on which elements of NOS were important to teach; only recently has there been an agreement on these important aspects (McComas, Almazroa, and Clough 1998). Schwartz, Lederman, and Crawford (2004) list seven aspects of NOS that define science as a discipline:

1. Scientific knowledge is subject to change.
2. Knowledge is empirically based.
3. Knowledge is theory laden and subjective.
4. Knowledge is the product of human imagination and creativity.
5. Knowledge involves the combination of observation and inferences.
6. Laws and theories play an important role in developing new ideas.

7. Scientific ideas, are validated by repetition and peer reviewing.

These seven aspects serve as the foundation for how science operates.

Helping students develop informed views of NOS has been an important goal for science education (Abd-El-Khalick, Bell, and Lederman 1998). There have been several attempts to enhance students' NOS views, but a valid instrument to assess NOS understanding was lacking for several years (Billeh and Hasan 1975). Recently, tools for gauging NOS have been developed, with many of them being multiple-choice surveys. Lederman, in conjunction with other researchers, has developed an open-ended instrument called the Views of Nature of Science Questionnaire (VNOS). This test has been proven to provide meaningful assessment of students' NOS views, as students are able to elucidate their own views of the target NOS aspect. Bell (1999) assessed the validity of this exam and found respondents with assessed thorough understanding of NOS scored much differently from individuals with assessed naive understandings. Individuals of the expert group all had doctoral degrees in science or science education; members of the novice group had similar educations, but their doctorates were in American literature or history. Data analyses indicated that the expert groups' responses to current NOS understandings were at a rate nearly three times higher than the novice group (Lederman et al. 2002). These results show a strong validity for the VNOS conceptual exam. Sample questions from VNOS (B) are provided in Figure 1.

FIGURE 1. Typical questions from VNOS

1. After scientists have developed a theory (e.g., atomic theory), does the theory ever change? If you believe that theories do change, explain why we bother to teach scientific theories. Defend your answer with examples.
2. What does an atom look like? How certain are scientists about the nature of the atom? What specific evidence do you think scientists use to determine what an atom looks like?

The nature of science is a term used to refer to epistemological commitments underlying the activities of science (Bell, Lederman, and Abd-El-Khalick 2000). Using NOS as a form of assessment is a relatively new idea in science classrooms, with some educators suggesting that a student's understanding of NOS is more important than their final course grades. Instructors often encourage students to learn intricate details, and although students may memorize these fine points, they forget them soon after taking the final exam. Should it not be more important to convey the most basic scientific principles and processes, rather than requiring students to memorize the obscure particulars? Assessing NOS levels in classrooms can help instructors mold their teaching strategies to better convey NOS aspects and raise students' understanding of science.

References

Abd-El-Khalick, F., R. L. Bell, and N. G. Lederman. 1998. The nature of science and instructional practice: Making the unnatural natural. *Science Education* 36: 404–420.

Anastasiow, N. J., G. D. Borich, T. M. Leonhardt, and S. A. Sibley. 1970. A comparison of guided discovery, discovery, and didactic teaching of math to kindergarten poverty children. *American Educational Research Journal* 7 (4): 493–510.

Bell, R. L. 1999. Understandings of the nature of science and decision making on science and technology based issues. Unpublished PhD dis. Oregon State University, Oregon.

Bell, R. L., I. Binns, and L. Smetana 2005. Simplifying inquiry instruction. *The Science Teacher*: 72 (7): 30–33.

Bell, R. L., N. G. Lederman, and F. Adb-El-Khalick. 2000. Developing and acting upon one's conception of the nature of science: A follow up study. *Journal of Research in Science Teaching* 37 (6): 563–581.

Billeh, V. Y., and O. E. Hasan. 1975. Factors influencing teachers' gain in understanding the nature of science. *Journal of Research in Science Teaching* 12: 209–212.

Lederman, N. G., F. Abd-El-Khalick, R. L. Bell, and R. S. Schwartz. 2002. Views of nature of science questionnaire: Toward valid and meaningful assessment of learners' conceptions of nature of science. *Journal of Research in Science Teaching* 39: 497–521.

McComas, W. F., H. Almazroa, and M. P. Clough. 1998. The nature of science in science education: An introduction. *Science and Education* 7: 511–532.

Schwartz, R. S., N. G. Lederman, and B. A. Crawford. 2004. Developing views of nature of science in an authentic context: An explicit approach to bridging the gap between nature of science and scientific inquiry. *Science Education* 88: 610–645.

Travis, H. J., and T. R. Lord. 2004. Traditional and constructivist teaching techniques: comparing two groups of undergraduate non-science majors in a biology lab. *Journal of College Science Teaching*: 34 (3): 12–18.

Chapter 13

Authentic Assessment: Using 5-E Lesson Plan Development to Evaluate Science Content Learning With Preservice Teachers

Holly Travis
Department of Biology
Indiana University of Pennsylvania
Indiana, Pennsylvania

Introduction

In recent years, the value of using authentic assessments to evaluate student learning has been discussed at all levels: elementary, secondary, and post-secondary. To be authentic, *assessment* should mirror application of the assessed ability in real-world, nonacademic settings. *Authentic assessments* turn lifeless rote learning into dynamic, functional information requiring students to apply their learning in life-based situations (Davies and Wavering 1999). By encouraging real-life applications of content, authentic assessments help students understand the value and applicability of the course material. This is just as true of preservice teachers, both primary and secondary, as it is with other students. With education students, however, application of content knowledge such as science, mathematics, or social studies means knowing how to use this knowledge to improve learning in their own classrooms. This has proven successful with Environmental Biology for Elementary Educators, the life science content course for preservice elementary teachers at Indiana University of Pennsylvania. By having students develop inquiry-based lessons using the 5-E model, it is possible to evaluate student mastery of content while developing confidence and demonstrating practical application of the information covered in class.

One aspect of lesson plan development that causes consternation among students is how to

Chapter 13

Authentic Assessment: Using 5-E Lesson Plan Development to Evaluate Science Content Learning With Preservice Teachers

write a lesson plan that incorporates inquiry and critical thinking skills, especially in science classes where they may already feel overwhelmed by the content they are covering in class. Educational research across many fields suggests the value of instruction that is less teacher-directed, with students exploring new ideas in context and engaging in more cooperative learning experiences (NRC 1996). By introducing preservice teachers from elementary, middle, and secondary levels to a simple model that infuses the inquiry method into the lesson plan format, the teachers find that concerns about the details disappear as they develop activities that fit the different sections of the model. The 5-E learning cycle is a template for lesson planning that addresses both content and inquiry standards, leading to increased student learning and decreased teacher stress (Rillero 1999).

The 5-E instructional scheme was developed by Trowbridge and Bybee (1990) as a means of easily creating a student-centered lesson. It is made up of five basic sections—*engage, explore, explain, elaborate* or *extend,* and *evaluate*—although these sections can be repeated within a lesson as needed to cover the required material. The 5-E model aids the instructor in maintaining a smooth flow during a class by giving a simple outline for developing the class procedures. It reduces time spent on unrelated topics and helps keep student groups on task. It also aids in developing better understanding of the material by encouraging students to explore new information before the explanation and by encouraging a variety of assessment techniques. Teachers will guide, focus, challenge, and encourage student learning as they move through the five steps of the lesson (Wilder and Shuttleworth 2005).

By combining the 5-E lesson plan format with the development of science lessons, preservice teachers learn how to effectively apply the information they are learning in class, becoming more confident in their ability to teach science and meet the demands for student-centered instruction. The lessons they generate on assigned topics

are then presented to classmates, taking advantage of the benefits of peer review and cooperative learning. In the process of crafting and sharing their lessons, the students also demonstrate an understanding of the science content covered in lecture and in lab activities.

Evaluating Content Knowledge

Content mastery is evaluated by analysis of the lesson plans and through peer comments during the lesson demonstrations. In order to show that the students have learned about agriculture, for example, lessons on soil types or integrated pest management might be required. The lessons are tied to the Pennsylvania State Standards for Environment and Ecology, and include all five parts of the 5-E model. A student who doesn't understand integrated pest management techniques and benefits will not be able to develop a lesson that clearly includes an *exploration* to activate prior learning and lead into the topic, an *explain* that involves the sharing of information from the first activity, and an *extension* requiring in-depth application of the topic being covered. In addition, evaluations included in the lesson plans must be varied and cover more than just memorization of facts and multiple-choice quizzes. A description of each section comprising a 5-E lesson and an example of a lesson on insects developed by a student are shown in Table 1.

Many environmental science topics lend themselves well to this type of evaluation. The water cycle, ecosystem interactions, trophic levels, biomes, and energy are just a few themes that have been evaluated using lesson plans. *Engage* suggestions very often incorporate children's literature, so language arts standards are met, as well. *Explore* activities could involve diagramming the water cycle or observing plants and animals that can be found near the school. In order to *explain* what they have done, children might be asked to share their observations or describe their diagrams and definitions. The *elaborate,* which

TABLE 1. 5-E description and sample lesson

	Description	Example from a lesson designed by a preservice elementary teacher
Engage	A brief activity, question, demonstration, or film "snippet" that whets the students' appetite and gets their attention focused on the topic.	Prepare "Ants on a Log" (celery with peanut butter and raisins, making sure no students are allergic to peanut butter); read Ant Cities by Arthur Dorros.
Explore	An activity in which the students develop questions and attempt to answer them, or challenge questions that encourage the students to think in depth about the topic.	Using ant farms, have students make observations about how the ants look and what they do.
Explain	Groups share their results, whether they have done an experiment or worked through a question. At this point, the teacher can also clear up misconceptions and misinformation to ensure that students understand the material.	The groups would take turns sharing their observations with the class, giving the teacher an opportunity to discuss functions and incorporate terminology.
Elaborate	Groups might do further laboratory work, do research, give presentations, or simply discuss more complex questions within their groups, allowing them to build a deeper understanding and to relate this information to other material covered in class.	Student groups go outside and observe ants in their natural habitat, making sketches of the things they observe. The groups would then return to the classroom and share their drawings and observations, comparing these with the things they saw in the ant farms.
Evaluate	Evaluation can take numerous forms, including standard quizzes or tests, written assignments, oral presentations, student self-evaluations, or observation of student participation in group activities.	Students can compare ants with other types of insects and tell how they are similar and different or identify why ants are an important part of the ecosystem.

should build on topics introduced earlier, might include building a model of the water cycle or making connections between organisms observed earlier to understand the interrelatedness of the ecosystem. Lessons then call for activities such as presentations, models, or creative writing assignments as the *evaluation*.

Creation of these lessons, with the attention to the objectives for each step, clearly demonstrates not only mastery of the content, but also an understanding of how to apply this in the classroom. As an added benefit, these lessons can easily integrate mathematics and language arts standards, making it easier for these preservice teachers to visualize their use in a classroom. Using children's literature, measuring and graphing, and writing journal entries are all things that have been used in lessons developed for class.

Chapter 13

Authentic Assessment: Using 5-E Lesson Plan Development to Evaluate Science Content Learning With Preservice Teachers

Conclusion

The use of authentic assessments, in the form of lesson plans, has proven to be a valuable tool for the evaluation of content mastery in preservice education classes. Not only do students feel that they are building a portfolio of useful ideas for their student teaching and future classroom use; they also demonstrate knowledge of the important features of major topics through the development of inquiry-based 5-E lessons. One preservice elementary teacher observed that the 5-E model improves learning because the students will remember more if they figure things out for themselves. What the preservice teachers don't often realize is that these lessons also improve their *own* learning through the practical application of course material. The Pennsylvania State Standards demand more than scientific processes such as observing, inferring, and experimenting. Instead, students should be engaging in activities that foster inquiry, including making observations, asking questions, testing hypotheses, and communicating their ideas to other people (NRC 1996). The 5-E model encourages these types of activities, both through their development in a college science content course and through their subsequent use in an elementary classroom.

References

Davies, M. A., and M. Wavering. 1999. *Alternative assessment: New directions in teaching and learning. Contemporary Education* 71 (1).

Duran, L. 2003. Investigating brine shrimp. *Science Activities* 40 (2): 30–34.

National Research Council (NRC). 1996. *National science education standards*. Washington, DC: National Academy Press.

Rillero, P. 1999. *Raphanus sativus*, germination and inquiry: A learning cycle approach for novice experimenters. *Electronic Journal of Science Education* 3 (4). (ERIC Document Reproduction Service No. EJ651190).

Trowbridge, L., and R. Bybee. 1990. *Becoming a secondary school science teacher* (5th ed.). Englewood Cliffs, NJ: Merrill.

Wilder, M., and P. Shuttleworth. 2005. Cell inquiry: A 5-E learning cycle lesson. *Science Activities* 41 (4): 36–43.

SECTION a

How-To-Section

Successful Classroom-Tested
Practices and Instructions and
Rubrics for Their Implementation

Chapter 14

Formative Assessment With Student Remotes and E-mail

Robert A. Cohen
Department of Physics
East Stroudsburg University
East Stroudsburg, Pennsylvania

Two formative assessment techniques were implemented in several sections of the first semester of the algebra-based introductory physics sequence at East Stroudsburg University, and the performance of those students was compared to sections in which the techniques were not implemented. It was found that the techniques had a positive impact on student learning.

Description

The following two formative assessment techniques were implemented as part of an introductory physics class (first semester of a two-semester sequence taken by life science majors, usually in their junior year):

1. Students were required to buy infrared response pads (eInstruction Corp.) that were used during class to assess student understanding and guide instruction. To build consensus among student answers to group quesions, students were encouraged to talk to their peers and explain the rationale for their answers, particularly for those questions where an initial polling did not reveal a consensus. Additional time was then spent on those areas that produced a lack of consensus or low success. This activity was designed to do the following:

   a. Allow students to get a sense of where they stood relative to the rest of the class.

b. Provide the instructor with a sense of how well the students were meeting the lesson objectives and thus allow the instructor to adapt instruction to student needs.

2. By putting into words the reasons for their choices, students were forced to examine the extent of their understanding (rather than re-gurgitation of facts and figures). Students were required to e-mail the instructor before each class with questions about the readings. The lessons were then designed to address those questions. This activity was designed to do the following:

a. Force students to focus on the extent of their understanding while reading the ma-terial.

b. Provide the instructor with insight into the areas in which students were experiencing difficulty so that the instructor could ad-dress those areas during class time. This aspect is similar to the Just-in-Time Teach-ing (JiTT) method discussed by Novak and his colleagues in 1999.

Neither activity was a requirement for the course. However, the participation rate was deter-mined and incorporated into a "bonus" that was added to the exam grade. The size of the bonus was determined not only by the participation rate but also by the exam score, such that higher exam scores warranted lower bonuses. The participa-tion rate itself was based upon how many times students utilized the remote in class, not whether the in-class answers were correct or not, and the number and quality of the e-mail questions.

The first technique can be implemented in a class of any size. The E-instruction bookstore model was used here, where students buy the remotes from the bookstore and register them online (which requires a small fee). Information about each student and their remotes is automati-cally recorded by the software. It requires some time up front to learn the software, set up the class information, and create the in-class questions for the first offering of the class (although ideas for these questions can be generated from the ques-tions students e-mail prior to class). Preparation for future classes is generally minimal. The sec-ond technique is probably only feasible in a class with 40 students or less. For example, with a 50% participation rate, the instructor of a 40-student class would need to read through 20 e-mails prior to each lesson and use those e-mails to construct the lesson. As implemented in this study, each e-mail was answered with a short response after the lesson. The time required to respond was typi-cally about 30 minutes to an hour, depending on the length of the responses. However, it is not clear that any response, let alone a lengthy one, is needed. Instructors of larger sections may be able to implement the second technique without answering the e-mails.

Effectiveness

To evaluate the effectiveness of these techniques, a short 17-question multiple-choice survey was given to several sections of the class, about half of which did not utilize the formative assessment techniques. Questions were selected from those that students typically are expected to answer correctly (i.e., they cover seemingly basic ideas of physics) but don't. The survey was also constructed with an eye toward making the survey as short as possible to simplify its administration. Each class received the instrument twice, at the beginning of the semester and at the end. It was found that the relative gain was consistently better in the classes that utilized the formative assessment techniques. More information regarding the evaluation of the survey data can be provided upon request.

Chapter 15

Peer Assessment: Value, Fears, Headaches, and Success

Anne Coleman
Department of Life and Physical Sciences
Cabrini College
Radnor, Pennsylvania

The idea of peer assessment sounds fantastic. The literature tells us that peer assessment is invaluable, and yet when most faculty first try peer assessment they are faced with a different reality. The promises of peer assessment are lofty. The literature tells us that through the use of peer assessment, learning will be facilitated because students are actively engaged in the management of their learning (Butler and Winne 1995). Because peers are assessing each other, final quality of work improves (through the power of peer pressure and formative assessment). Students that are engaged in peer assessment develop better critical thinking skills due to the engagement in evaluation of peer work (Haas and Keeley 1998). In the larger picture, peer evaluation is supposed to make our students more marketable. Through peer assessment students are obtaining and sharpening skills needed for managerial positions, which require providing constructive feedback to others and fairly evaluating performance without bias. Peer assessment of group work is supposed to hone students' abilities to work in teams because through peer assessment they have learned how to work effectively and productively within a diverse team framework (Mello 1993). And finally through peer assessment the ability to self-critique is enhanced and therefore improves one's own work output.

If all this were true and easily accomplished the majority of faculty in every discipline would be embracing this strategy and incorporating it

Section

3

into every class, but for most, this has not been the reality, at least not at first. For those faculty willing to try peer assessment, the obstacles abound. First, there is the initial obstacle of just trying the technique. It is new and different and we as faculty tend to be like everyone else: We do what we experienced as learners way back when. Peer assessment is new territory that comes with risks (Haas and Keeley 1998). The risks include what administrators, department chairs, and peers may think. Many are not always supportive of faculty who want to experiement with new pedagogy, particularly if parents start calling to complain. The risks also involve the students and how they will or will not embrace the idea of their peers having a role in assessment. For many students the concept of true peer assessment is foreign to them in the academic arena, and students have misconceptions and fear about peer assessment. This may be particularly true for students who are not confident in their skills. Such trepidation if not handled well may have an impact on student evaualtions. This in turn could impact tenure and promotion decisions depending on the institution.

Apart from how students' reactions impact the faculty member, students have their own fears and concerns. Most of their concerns center on grades and "fairness." They want to be assured that if they put significant effort into a project, they will get credit for their effort and that someone who just threw their project together is not going to receive the same grade (Conway et al. 1993; Hanrahan and Issacs 2001). They may also see the process as a waste of their time and/or not part of their "job." This may come from their perception, right or wrong, that their opinion really does not matter to the professor or their peers. As a result they may blow off the responsibility, citing that it does not matter because they are not going to be held directly accountable for the quality of their evaluation (Higgins, Hartley, and Skelton 2002). Another result often is that students will simply see this as an opportunity for grade boosting or as an opportunity to gang up on the "curve buster." A more sensitive concern is that of con-

fidentiality. Students who are struggling may not want to put that out there for peers to see.

The principal obstacle is correct implementation of the technique. The first step of implementation is deciding on the desired outcome of the peer assessment. What do you want the peer assessment to accomplish? Is the goal to gain a general feedback on a presentation/product from the entire class, a segment of the class, or on one to one basis? Or is the peer assessment about participation on a group project? Is the assessment formative with the hopes that the student will use the feedback to make changes before the final product? What level of feedback is desired? Simple Lickert scales or comments or edits? Is the assessment going to be part of the grade for the assessed or the assessor? If one or both parties gets a grade, how much of the total? Is the feedback going to be anonymus? If so, how is that going to be accomplished? Is it going to be a computer form with no ID attached or handwritten and then tabulated by whom? Is the assessment formative or summative?

Once the outcomes have been established the next step is actual implementation in the classroom. There have been a number of investigations on the best practices of peer assessment (Gueldenzoph and May 2002; Conway et al. 1993; Lejk 1996; Goldfinch and Raeside 1990). From that literature the same basic best practices emerge, regardless of discipline or type of assessment:

1. Peer evaluation needs to be made an integral part of the course so that the culture of peer assessment can be firmly established. If peer assessment is to be taken seriously, students have to be comfortable with the concept and practice of the method, and that comes with use.

2. Clarification of guidelines and expectations need to be communicated to the students. This includes specifically articulating exactly who evaluates whom, what the level of anonymity is, what the evaluation includes, when

the evaluation occurs, why the evaluation occurs and what impact the evaluation has on grades.

3. Students should have input into the evaluation criteria. There is greater buy in from the students if the students have helped develop the criteria particularly when it comes to assessing individuals of a group. Most educational researchers recommend having each group decide on its own rules by which each member will be judged. For example, the group may decide that missing a group meeting will automatically result in a reduction of a specific number of points. Another group may focus on deadlines. Allowing the group members decide increases buy in to the peer assessment.

4. The evaluation needs to be effective, which means that except in cases of formative peer assessment it must be quantifiable (Conway et al. 1993) and, with few exceptions, anonymous. For example asking, "Was the member a good team player?" is not measurable, but asking, "On a scale of 1–5 with 1 being 'never' and 5 being 'always,' how often was the group member present and contributing to group meetings?" is quantifiable. Having specific tools increases the chances of honest participation (Lejk 1996). This is not to say that qualitative assessments are not valuable or needed. Qualitative assessments have been demonstrated to be invaluable to the individual but are difficult to incorporate into a grade.

5. If possible, formative assessment should be incorporated into the peer assessment so that students can make adjustments to their behavior/performance/product over time. Giving students that ongoing type of check-in increases motivation and improves work quality and communication skills (Frank and Barzilai 2004; Prins et al. 2005).

6. If grade inflation is a concern, best practices seem to fall into two categories: composing a final grade that includes both peer assessment and faculty assessment, or limiting the points the peers have to disperse to those they are evaluating. For example, Clyde Freeman Herreid from State University of New York at Buffalo suggests for group-member evaluations that the team members have a maximum number of points to distribute across the group members, and if a student awards more or less points to specific students, they have to justify it.

After several failed ventures into peer assessment, during which grade distribution across peer assessment was less than a 6% spread with and without careful clarification of the rubric, a new approach was needed. So after talking to students, it became clear that money was a big motivator and something students did not readily want to give up. An idea was born: The project was called "Donations Please."

The original peer assessments were left in the course. These included anonymous class peers assessments of oral presentations on "hot topics." The rubric included several categories: appropriateness of topic choice, communication with the audience, clear expression of ideas, and projection of material retention. Students also had two opportunities to assess group members on two different projects—a reservation design and an Amazon stakeholder case. For the group member evaluation there was a limit on the number of total points that could be assigned, and a reason was required for additional or reduced number of points. As in the past, the point spread was less than 4% for the hot topic assessments and 10% for the group peer assessment. The rationale for keeping the original assessments was to establish a culture of peer assessment. The final peer assessment was part of a culminating project. Each student chose an ecology issue about which they were passionate. Topics included hybrid cars, acid rain, recycling, invasive species, and Christmas trees. The project had two products—a tri-fold poster presentation and a formal paper. The students were instructed that they needed to become experts on their topics and that the goal of the tri-fold poster presentations was to raise money for their causes. To do this they needed to prepare to answer questions from peers and outside "donors" and develop arguments for different audiences to justify why their cause deserved donations. Prior to the presentation day, students were walked through the schedule of the presentations and the evaluation method, which involved receiving and giving donations. They were also told the areas of expertise that the outsiders represented.

The day of the presentation the students were randomly placed into three groups. The reason for the division on the day of the presentations was to decrease the likelihood of coalitions forming. One-third of the class presented at a time. Each student was given a clip of money (Claus dollars) to use for donation purposes. The catch was that each student was given only enough money so that if they equally distributed it, the resulting grade would be a 90%. Students were also told that they did not have to give out all of their money. Some time was spent prior to the day of presentations and then again on the day, explaining the expectations of the assessment and the value of being truthful in that assessment. The outside visitors were then introduced to the class. They included administrators, staff, and other faculty members. They acted as philanthropists, each with a specific focus (businessperson, concerned doctors of the world, venture capitalist, EPA grant administrator, wealthy tree-hugger type, and Hollywood star). Students were told that if a philanthropist was convinced to donate money to their cause, they would earn extra credit. (Their money was a different color and was placed into jars in the same way as the student donations.)

The fun then began. One-third of the class set up their posters and the other two-thirds of the class walked around, asked questions, and evaluated the tri-fold poster presentations. To help preserve anonymity and increase chances of fair assessments, the donation jars were placed behind a screen so neither the presenters nor the other donors knew how much each person was donating. The grades are based on the average donation amount.

This project has been run twice and was successful each time on several fronts. Grade distribution increased dramatically to a 30% point spread, which was a much better reflection of the scope of the quality of the presentations. Using money donations for the peer assessment instead of circling scores and writing short comments appeared to increase the criticalness of the evaluations, and since improved communication skills equaled higher quality of final product, students took it seriously.

References

Conway, R., D. Kember, A. Sivan, and M. Wu. 1993. Peer assessment of an individual's contribution to a group project. *Assessment and Evaluation in Higher Education* 18 (1): 45–56.

Frank, M., and A. Barzilai. 2004. Integrating alternative assessment in a project-based learning course for preservice science and technology teachers. *Assessment and Evaluation in Higher Education* 29 (1): 41–61.

Goldfinch, J., and R. Raeside. 1990. Development of peer assessment technique for obtaining individual marks on a group project. *Assessment and Evaluation in Higher Education* 15 (3): 210–231.

Gueldenzoph, L. E., and G. L. May. 2002. Collaborative peer evaluation: Best practices for group member assessments. *Business Communication Quarterly* 65 (1): 9–20.

Haas, P., and S. Keeley. 1998. Coping with faculty resistance to teaching critical thinking. *College Teaching* 46 (2): 63–67.

Hanrahan, S. J., and G. Issacs. 2001. Assessing self- and peer-assessment: The student's views. *Higher Education Research and Development* 20 (1): 53–70.

Higgins, R., P. Hartley, and A. Skelton. 2002. The conscientious consumer: Reconsidering the role of assessment in student learning. *Studies in Higher Education* 27 (1): 53–64.

Lejk, M. 1996. A survey of methods of deriving individual grades from group assessment. *Assessments and Evaluation in Higher Education* 21 (3): 267–280.

Mello, J. A. 1993. Improving individual member accountability in small work group settings. *Journal of Management Education* 17 (2): 253–259.

Prins, F. J., D. M. Sluijsmans, P. A. Kirshcner, and J. W. Strijbos. 2005. Formative peer assessment in a CSCL environment: A case study. *Assessment and Evaluation in Higher Education* 30 (4): 117–144.

Chapter 16

Working With Student Engagement

Grace Eason
Science and Science Education
University of Maine at Farmington
Farmington, Maine

"Classroom Assessment informs teachers how effectively they are teaching and students how effectively they are learning" (Cross 1996). For this purpose I constructed an assessment tool known as the Diagnostic Learning Log (DLL) for my introductory biology course, based on suggestions by Angelo and Cross in the early 1990s. The DLL is a focused journal entry where students indicate what they have learned from a particular unit, pose questions, identify aspects of classroom practice they found helpful, and provide suggestions for facilitating their own understanding of the subject matter. The DLL provides an instructor with in-depth information and insight into students' thinking skills and awareness of their own learning, and allows students to document, diagnose, and determine a course of action to better their learning in specific classes (Eason 2006). The DLL can be posted online or distributed to students in class. I allow students to complete three online DLL entries per semester, which are posted on my Blackboard site. Students post an entry after each unit of instruction and are given 10 points for answering all of the DLL questions (See Figure 1, p.96). The three entries for the semester total approximately 8% of their overall grade. I find this an invaluable tool when I am experimenting with a variety of different strategies in my science courses. Some of those strategies include role-playing, BSCS 5E activities, small-group work, and various forms of class discussion techniques.

This tool is extremely flexible and the DLL questions can be altered to suit the instructor's preferences. For example, this past semester while I was teaching my introductory environmental science course, I wanted to investigate why my students thought a particular teaching strategy was effective. I decided to expand on a previous DLL question by asking students their level of engagement with the variety of teaching strategies I was using. Monitoring student engagement allows me to determine which teaching strategies capture the student's attention, in order to ensure that they are actively engaged with the concepts that are presented to them. In essence, that they find the information that they are learning relevant and meaningful. The manner in which informa-

---

FIGURE 1: Diagnostic Learning Log

This assignment is extremely important; it helps me to focus on what you need out of this course, and it also allows me to determine what changes need to be made for the future. In addition, since this is a discussion forum, I encourage you to review and respond to your classmates' answers. The feedback you receive from your peers may be extremely helpful. Please be honest and be as specific as possible. You may also provide feedback on what occurs in lab.

Diagnostic Log Question 1

List the main points you learned from this unit. Provide at least three examples.

Diagnostic Log Question 2

What are some questions that you still have regarding the information that was discussed within this unit of study?

Diagnostic Log Question 3

Please complete the following statements:
A. My understanding of the subject matter during this unit was most helped by

_____.

B. My understanding of the subject matter during this unit was most hindered by

_____.

Diagnostic Log Question 4

During this unit of study I found that (Choose one)

_____ Many different teaching approaches were used.
_____ Some different teaching approaches were used.
_____ Very few teaching approaches were used.

Examples of teaching approaches include lecture, partner and group discussions, whole class discussions, role-playing, demonstrations, audio and video transcripts, drawing, etc....)

What are your feelings about the teaching approaches used?

Diagnostic Log Question 5

Please complete the following statement:

Overall, the moments during this unit when I was most engaged, excited, and involved as a learner were when _____. Explain your response.

Diagnostic Log Question 6

Please complete the following statement:

Overall the moments during this unit when I was most distanced, disengaged, and uninvolved as a learner were when _____ Explain your response.

Diagnostic Log Question 7

Based on this unit of study, what suggestions do you have for changes that may facilitate your understanding of the subject matter?

---

tion is presented is the key to student engagement and there is a delicate balance between process and content. For example, small-group work can increase student motivation because learners have a greater opportunity to apply the concepts that they are learning. Students share their thoughts with group members and have the opportunity to mentor one another in understanding various scientific concepts. Occasionally, however, when attempting to truly analyze a concept, group consensus based on casual opinion can occur and instead of truly working to understand a concept, students often take the easy route and settle for whatever answer is most convenient. Asking a DLL questions such as "My understanding of the subject matter was most helped by _____" and "My understanding of the subject matter was most hindered by _____;" provides students with the opportunity to reflect on their learning processes while participating in a variety of class activities, including those activities that involve group work. The additional student engagement questions ask students about the variety of teaching methods I use and when they feel the most and least engaged.

Overall, the DLL is a very beneficial assessment tool in guiding my teaching practice. It enables me to obtain student feedback throughout the semester. This provides me with the opportunity to modify my instruction accordingly rather than waiting until the end of the semester for student evaluations. My students also benefit from the DLL because it provides them with an opportunity for reflection, and this empowers them to identify where the gaps are in their own learning and where they can begin to critically analyze how their learning is progressing.

References

Angelo, T. A., and K. P. Cross. 1993. *Classroom assessment techniques: A handbook for college teachers*. 2nd ed. San Francisco, CA: Jossey-Bass.

Cross, K. P. 1996. Classroom research: Implementing the scholarship of teaching. In *Classroom assessment and research: An update on uses, approaches, and research findings*, ed. T. Angelo, 5–12. San Francisco, CA: Jossey-Bass.

Eason, G. 2006. Is there room for reflection in a science course for non-science majors? *Journal of College Science Teaching* 35 (5): 37–41.

Chapter 17

Promoting Student Reflection on Exams

Grace Eason
Science and Science Education
University of Maine at Farmington
Farmington, Maine

One of the greatest challenges in assessing student performance is providing students with the detailed and appropriate feedback they need to learn from their mistakes. Summative assessments, in the form of exams, are used to determine what students have learned from a particular unit of instruction and oftentimes what they have learned throughout the entire semester. However, students have a tendency to focus only on the grade and not what they did correctly or incorrectly on the exam and why some answers were acceptable and others were not.

In order to encourage students in my introductory environmental science course (n=38) to use exams as a learning tool, I adapted a classroom assessment technique called the Exam Evaluation. This simple assessment "allows teachers to examine what students think they are learning from exams and tests. The evaluation can also provide the instructor with student reactions to tests and exams so that they can make the exams more effective as learning and assessment devices" (Angelo and Cross 1993). The Exam Evaluation is an optional assignment that contains a series of questions that students complete following each exam throughout the semester. Students have the option of completing the evaluation and receiving a maximum of five points, which they may apply to their exam score. There were three unit exams (50 points each) during the semester and one final exam. Students had the opportunity to complete exam evaluations for all three unit exams. The exam evaluation format can vary depending on what the instructor is focusing. My focus was on demonstrating that exams can be very effective in helping students monitor their learning throughout the course.

The first question asks students to describe content of the exam. This begins the reflective process, because students must think back and describe the main concepts covered in the exam. The second question asks students to give one or two examples of their successful responses and to explain what things they did that made these responses successful. By focusing on successful responses, students analyze what elements of their responses satisfy the question criteria and why the responses received full credit. The third question asks students to rewrite the question(s) that contained incorrect information. Any short answer or essay question responses must be correctly rewritten. This promotes another level of analysis—by going through the exam and addressing each incorrect response students not only discover what the correct answer is but they also reorganize and incorporate the correct information in short-answer and essay responses. The final question asks students what, if anything, could they do differently to be successful on the next exam? This is the final step in the reflective process and requires students to think about how they prepared for the exam and what steps to take in the future to be more successful. The responses that I have received to this question are very honest and illustrate students' reflective processes. Some example responses follow:

Because I am very aware that more work on my part would have produced a higher grade (due to better understanding of the material covered) I started immediately studying for the next test. It is not enough to read the material assigned (which I did do),

and answer assigned questions (which I also did). I must really make sure I understand the answers to the questions and can explain them to someone else. That illustrates a higher level of learning than just recall. I did great on the multiple-choice, however I did bad on the short-answer questions because I had to take that knowledge, apply it, and explain it back to you.

On the next test I really need to read the questions more carefully. When going back over my incorrect answers I was surprised to see that many of them I knew, it just took me reading the questions a few times, and really looking for what the question was asking. On my short answer questions I need to slow down a bit and make sure all of the information being asked of me is complete.

Student Survey Results

A survey was distributed to students at the end of the spring 2007 semester. The following results of the survey are only preliminary, since this is the first time that I have used this instrument. A total of 38 students completed the survey.

Question 1: How often did you complete an exam evaluation over the course of the semester?

    a. 3
    b. 2
    c. 1
    d. 0

A total of 26% (10 students) completed all three exam evaluations, 37% (14 students) completed two of the three evaluations, 16% (6 students) completed one exam evaluation, and 21% (8 students) did not complete any of the exam evaluations.

Question 2: If you answered 0 or 1 in question 1, please indicate why you did not complete an exam evaluation after each exam?

Fourteen students answered this question. Seven students indicated that they did not have the time due to too much work in other courses, and another seven students indicated that they felt their test grades were satisfactory and that they understood the concepts well enough.

Question 3: If you answered 2 or 3 in question 1, what motivated you to complete the exam evaluation?

Twenty-four students completed either two or three evaluations. Nineteen students indicated that they did it because it helped them learn from their mistakes and it improved their test grades. Three students indicated that they needed the extra points in case they did poorly on another assignment. Two students indicated that they were determined to do well in this course.

Question 4: In what ways did you find the exam evaluation helpful? (Circle all that apply.)

a. I was able to correct my incorrect answers and this helped me to further learn the material.

b. I was able to reflect on my exam responses and this helped me with my study strategies for future exams.

c. I was able to correct my incorrect answers but I did not learn from it. I just needed the points.

d. Other (Please complete)_____

Only students who completed two or three exam evaluations responded to this question. Twelve students indicated that the evaluations enabled them to correct their incorrect answers, which facilitated their learning of the material *and* also helped them reflect on their exam responses for future study strategies. Six students indicated that they were able to correct their incorrect responses and this helped them to further understand the material. Four students indicated that they were able to reflect on their exam responses and this helped them with their study strategies for future exams. Two students indicated that they were able to correct their incorrect answers but they did not learn from it. They just needed the points.

Question 5: Should I continue using the exam evaluation in future classes?

The twenty-four students that completed two or three exam evaluations indicated that I should continue using the exam evaluations in future classes. Of the fourteen students who completed only one exam evaluation or did not complete an exam evaluation, eight students commented that they appreciated having a choice to improve their exam scores. Six students indicated no response to this question.

I will continue to use this assessment tool in the future. I found it extremely helpful in promoting student reflection using examinations. I plan on modifying it to include additional questions that will help me make my exams more effective as a learning and assessment instrument. In addition, I will collect data on whether or not student exam scores improve on subsequent exams following the completion of an exam evaluation.

Reference

Angelo, T. A., and K. P. Cross. 1993. *Classroom assessment techniques: A handbook for college teachers.* 2nd ed. San Francisco, CA: Jossey-Bass.

Chapter 18

Hypothesis Modification Activity

Brian J. Rybarczyk
The Graduate School
University of North Carolina at Chapel Hill
Chapel Hill, North Carolina

Kristen Walton
Department of Biology
Missouri Western State University
St. Joseph, Missouri

Many upper-level undergraduate science courses are content and data laden, leaving little room for students to practice important skills such as generating hypotheses and designing experiments. The Hypothesis Modification Activity is a technique that engages students in forming their own hypotheses in response to an experimental question, provides an opportunity for students to consider different lines of evidence, and allows them to incorporate new knowledge into their thinking in a systematic way. This is a process-based technique that employs brainstorming, synthesis, and evaluation skills. The activity allows students opportunities for reflection, since students create a written record of their thought process over several class sessions. For instructors, this is a low-burden, easy-to-implement, high-impact, active-learning technique.

Implementation

Without delving into content, the instructor initially poses a testable research question related to a thematic unit being discussed. Students are given five minutes to generate a short list of hypotheses (3–4 ideas) that may answer the question. Initially, students typically propose hypotheses that are broad in scope and not well defined. Depending on the level of the students, they may need to be reminded that scientific hypotheses must be testable. Students are asked

Section

3

to save their lists and bring them to subsequent class meetings. Additional content is covered and students are given another five minutes to revise their initial hypotheses list or generate new hypotheses that incorporate new content just discussed. This process is repeated two or three times, depending on the length of time allotted to cover the topic. Students' final lists typically contain much more specific, testable hypotheses. After the final revision, students share their lists with two or three other students in a group. The group then chooses one hypothesis and designs an experiment to test it. The general process is outlined in Figure 1.

FIGURE 1. General process for group decision making

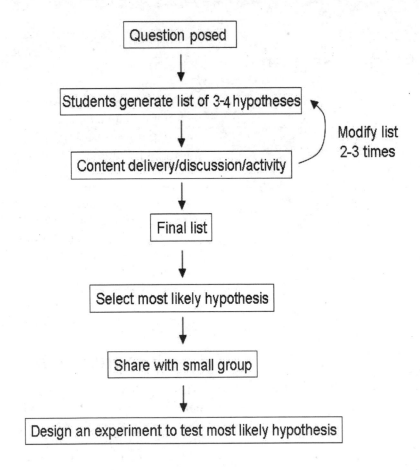

Any research question in any science discipline that represents a major concept, current topic, controversy, or dilemma could be used for this activity as a central focus for a series of class sessions. Some research questions could include the following:

- What biological hypotheses could explain why in clinical drug trials some drugs work for one group of people and not another group?
- What environmental influences could alter the evolution of an organism?
- What biological/immunological mechanisms are involved in how quickly a person progresses to a disease state?

Many students generate similar lists and incorporate knowledge discussed in class. Some students also have ideas for very different hypotheses by the end of the activity. These variations provide for rich discussions among the students.

Evaluation

From a preliminary evaluation survey, students agreed with the statements in Figure 2.

Comments from students included the following:

I thought this was a good activity because it asked you to continually reevaluate your knowledge on the subject and to apply this knowledge to the original question/situation. It helped me to organize my thoughts and think more critically about the scenario.

Of course I have been asked to formulate hypotheses in class before, but never on a progressive basis have I been asked to modify it as I learned more about a disease or other topic. This was a pretty cool way to document the learning process that I went through over the span of just a few class lectures.

This activity provides a unique opportunity for students to propose hypotheses that address a scientific question, modify their ideas, and incorporate new information, which are critical skills for scientific thinking.

FIGURE 2. Student agreement on evaluation

	% responses (n = 35)
I was able to propose viable hypotheses.	80.0%
I was able to evaluate each of my hypotheses and propose even better hypotheses each time I revisited my list.	71.4%
I learned alternative hypotheses from other students.	68.6%
I was able to synthesize information from class.	63.0%
It was a very helpful learning experience.	54.3%
I have been asked to formulate hypotheses in my other biology courses.	51.4%

Acknowledgments

This work was supported by the Seeding Post-doctoral Innovators in Research and Education (SPIRE) program, grant 5K12GM000678 from the National Institute of General Medical Sciences, a division of the National Institutes of Health.

Chapter 19

Exam Corrections and Analysis, Student Perspective

Kathryn H. Sorensen
Biology Department
American River College
Sacramento, California

One of the most difficult parts of being a teacher is giving exams back to students when you know, and the students know, that the students did not perform well. Being confronted by angry students in and out of the classroom is not fun for the instructor or for the other students in the class. Science classes tend to build on previous material. This means that if a student performs poorly on one exam, it may have repercussions on future exam scores.

Students also accuse instructors of being tricky or unfair on exams. To help combat this perception, as well as to help students take responsibility for their own scores and exam preparation, I have students perform exam corrections and analysis on their first two exams. Some of my colleagues use this on every exam.

The basic outline[1] is as follows:

A. For each question you <u>missed</u> on the exam:
  1. Restate or copy the question and correct answer.
  2. List the incorrect answer and explain why it cannot be correct.
  3. Explain why you missed the question:
     a. Misread or didn't understand question
     b. Used incorrect logic
     c. Didn't know enough information to answer the question

---

[1.] Modified from UM-Kansas City Supplemental Instruction Program documents.

B. For each question you answered <u>correctly</u>: Which of the following do you think helped you to answer the question correctly?

Section
3

   a. Previewed the assigned reading material before coming to lecture
   b. Attended all lectures
   c. Reviewed last lecture's notes before the next lecture
   d. Rewrote notes
   e. Integrated the lecture notes with the text
   f. Organized basic concepts using charts, lists, notes, tables, etc.
   g. Self-tested on material to be covered on the exam
   h. Prepared answers for the learning objectives
   i. Practiced explaining or "teaching" concepts to a friend (real or imaginary)
   j. Attend tutoring sessions
   k. Studied old tests and rearranged questions and predicted new questions
   l. Studied with friends
   m. Got extra help from the instructor, IA, or tutor
   n. Studied material regularly instead of cramming at the last minute
   o. Ate a meal prior to the exam
   p. Got ample sleep the night before the exam

The key to this analysis is threefold: (1) Students get a chance to take some time to go over the entire exam by themselves with all of their notes and text available. (2) Students have to look at the questions they missed as well as the questions they got right. Typically, they only want to focus on what they missed so that they can argue for points. This way, they have to look at the entire exam to see any patterns in their performance. Was there a section of the content that they absolutely didn't know? Did they miss class when the professor covered some material? (3) And finally, sing this analysis puts the onus of responsibility back on the student rather than on the professor. Students are often surprised how much material they have simply not paid attention to while studying.

Chapter 20

Exam Analysis, Instructor Perspective

Kathryn H. Sorensen
Biology Department
American River College
Sacramento, California

In chapter 19, I mentioned that I think one of the most difficult parts of being a teacher is giving exams back to students when you know, and the students know, that the students did not perform well. In this teaching tip, I address what I think is *the* most difficult job of an instructor: effectively assessing what our students have learned. I think most of us can articulate what we want our students to know at the end of a unit or class, but devising questions that help us measure whether or not they have is extremely difficult. When I ask faculty if they have analyzed their own exams, very few of them have given it any thought.

The best exam writer I have ever known is now-retired biology instructor Dr. Judith Edmiston from the University of Texas at Austin. Her exams are legendary in the department for their length and difficulty (which she liked to refer to as "rigor"; however, what I came to appreciate about them was the thoughtfulness with which she composed them. As her teaching assistant (TA) for two and a half years, this appreciation took some time to develop since I had to grade them!

One required class for biology TAs introduced us to a variety of teaching methods and activities that we could use in our discussion sections. One of those activities involved an analysis of an exam by the instructor for whom we worked. The rubric we used was Bloom's Taxonomy (see chapter 8, page 49). The rubric suggests that there are a variety of ways we can construct

Section

3

questions, from low-level expectation (knowledge, comprehension) to high-level expectation (synthesis, evaluation). As I evaluated Dr. Edmiston's exams, I realized that there was a mix of all six levels of the taxonomy. This surprised me as she taught the first semester introductory-level biology course. I asked her about this result, and the discussion that followed changed forever the way I wrote exams and, more importantly, how I structured my classes.

She claimed that the activity we were doing in evaluating the exams was only half the story. She had me pull out the notes I took in her class (yes, she made the TAs attend class and take notes along with the students), and as we walked through the notes and handouts, it was easy to see where her questions came from. One thing that she kept telling me was that the students needed to *practice* the types of questions that they would see on the exams. She felt this was true for all levels of questions, whether simple or more difficult. She provided old exams and a variety of handouts to help students practice for the types of questions they could expect on exams. This helped prepare students in an introductory-level course to answer high-level questions.

I hope my students do their part in preparing for exams, and I want to hold myself to a high standard as well. I encourage you to take an hour to evaluate your exams. Then, take awhile to see if what you do in your class matches what you expect from your students on exams. You may be surprised. I know that I have been.

Chapter 21

Inquiry-Based Labs: The Scientific Report

Bonnie S. Wood
Biology Department
University of Maine at Presque Isle

In my General Biology I course, five inquiry-based laboratories occur during appropriate weeks of the semester. At the beginning of each of these laboratories, students practice a general protocol and are given a list of available materials. With their cooperative learning team, the students then design and conduct their own experiments. The learning group must state a clear hypothesis and describe its materials and methods to me before starting its experiment. Although all four group members participate in the experiment and are expected to understand relevant content, a different student is responsible for writing the scientific report for each inquiry-based laboratory and that student is graded individually on his or her report. Adherence to the scientific method is stressed, and the report is written in the style of a peer-reviewed journal article. At least two days before submitting the final report to me, students must review their draft, with peer tutors in the Writing Center. Although this is an introductory biology course for both majors and nonmajors, students are very engaged in the scientific process and, if they carefully follow the Scientific Report of Laboratory Investigation Grading Criteria (Table 1, p. 112), generally produce excellent papers.

Section
3

TABLE 1. Scientific Report of Laboratory Investigation Grading Criteria Biology I

(Distribution of points as described below)

First Author's Name: _____

Topic of Laboratory Exercise: _____

Signature of Writing Center Tutor: _____

Date of Writing Center Consultation: _____

TOTAL POINTS OUT OF 30 = _____

TITLE AND AUTHORS

2   Title is written at the top of the report (not on a cover sheet) and is descriptive, concise, and appropriate in tone and structure for a scientific journal. Title allows reader to anticipate the experimental design. You are listed as the first author with contributing learning group members listed as second, third, and fourth authors.

1   Title is descriptive but does not allow the reader to anticipate the experiment design. Names of authors are incomplete or misspelled.

0   Title and authors are on a separate cover sheet; title is the same as the general topic of the laboratory exercise (as given in the coursepack).

GENERAL CONSIDERATIONS

2   All material is placed in the correct sections as described below and organized logically within each section; the organization runs parallel among the different sections. The report is neatly typed, single-spaced, with correct spelling and grammar. Pages are numbered in the upper right corners. The entire report is in paragraph form. All measurements are in SI units with proper abbreviations; genus and species are underlined or italicized with genus capitalized. Underlining in the text is not done for any other purposes (as for emphasis).

1   The materials are placed in the correct sections, all of which are written in paragraph form, but the report does not have a neat appearance, or contains frequent errors of spelling and grammar, or does not use SI units or correctly write genus and species of organisms.

0   As for 1 but the materials are incorrectly located in the sections or the sections are missing.

ABSTRACT

3   Is 100 words or less and contains the purpose of the experiment, a brief description of methods, results, and conclusions.

2   Is lacking one of the elements listed for 3 and/or is too long or too short.

1   Is lacking more than one of the elements listed for 3 and/or is too long or too short.

0   Abstract missing or does not contain the elements listed for 3.

INTRODUCTION

5   Contains background information from the literature (primary references) that directly relate to the experiment. The in-text citation form is correct and citations are paraphrased (quotation marks are not used). Purpose of the experiment and your hypothesis are clearly stated. Information from the coursepack is not copied, but rather the topic is described in your own words, using information you have learned in Biology 112, both in class and from your own reading.

4   As for 5 but background information from the literature is lacking, along with citations.

3   As for 4, but purpose or the hypothesis are lacking.

2   As for 3, but both purpose and hypothesis are lacking.

1   Information in the Introduction belongs in another section of the report.

0   Introduction is missing or is not written in your own words.

MATERIALS AND METHODS

5   The materials are described in paragraph form (not listed like ingredients in a recipe). Section is written in past tense and contains all relevant information, in an appropriate chronology to enable a reader to repeat the experiment. The exact procedure you actually followed is described, not necessarily what was written in the coursepack. Information is complete enough so everything in the rest of the report can be related back to Materials and Methods, but the section avoids unnecessary, wordy descriptions of procedures. Precise measurements are given using SI units.

4   As for 5, but contains unnecessary or wordy descriptions.

3   As for 5, but gives sequential information in a disorganized, confusing way.

2   Describes an experiment that is marginally replicable, so the reader must infer parts of the basic design. The procedures are not quantitatively described.

1   Describes the experiment so poorly or in such a nonscientific way that it cannot be replicated. Contains information that belongs in a different section.

0   Materials and Methods section is missing or is not written in your own words.

RESULTS

5   Contains quantifiable experimental data with the units clearly defined and labeled in both text and graphics. Drawings, graphs, and tables are included where appropriate. Figure captions are placed below the figure; table captions above the table. Figure and table captions are informative and can be understood independently of the text. Results are described in paragraph form in the text and the text refers to each table and figure. Your actual results are described, rather than extrapolations or what you should have gotten (save this for Discussion). No explanation is given for the results.

4   As for 5, but figure and table captions cannot be understood without reading the text.

3   As for 4, but the data reported in the text, the graphs, or the tables include information that is irrelevant to the purpose of the experiment or the hypothesis.

2   Quantifiable experimental data are present, but the quantities or intervals are inappropriate or information is not displayed graphically when appropriate.

1   The section does not contain or communicate quantifiable results. The information belongs in another section of the report.

0   The Results section is missing.

Section
3

DISCUSSION

5 Both observed and expected results are summarized, including a statement of why you think you got the results presented in the Results section. Errors and inconsistencies in procedure are pointed out. Possible explanations of unexpected results are given as well as suggestions for further and/or improved experimentation. A statement of whether the hypothesis is accepted or rejected is made by comparing your hypothesis with the data.

4 As for 5, but accepting or rejecting the hypothesis is lacking.

3 As for 4, but suggestions for further and/or improved experimentation are lacking.

2 As for 3, but unexpected results are ignored.

1 The results are summarized but are not interpreted.

0 The Discussion section is missing.

REFERENCES

3 References are primary journal articles, textbooks or peer-reviewed internet sources (i.e., from a journal, not from a source like Wikipedia). References, listed using American Psychological Association (APA) style, are correct, complete, and consistent. All references have been cited in the text (authors' names and dates) and all citations in the text have been included in the References section. The reference list is arranged in alphabetical order according to the first author's surname. First names are given as initials.

2 As for 3, but consistent APA style is not used.

1 As for 2, but some references are inappropriate (i.e. are not from primary journal articles, textbooks or peer-reviewed internet sources) or are not cited in the text or citations in the text are not included in the References section.

0 The References section is missing.

Chapter 22

Student-Authored Book Reviews

Bonnie S. Wood
Biology Department
University of Maine at Presque Isle

In every science course I teach (both general education core and upper level), students choose and read a book available in the campus library. The separate book list I provide for each course comprises books that relate to the specific topics covered in that course. I chose these books for the library based on reviews I read over the years in journals such as *Science News, Scientific American, The New York Times Book Review, Journal of College Science Teaching,* and *The American Biology Teacher.* The student's review describes the appropriateness of this book for someone taking the course in which they are enrolled. At least one week before submitting the final paper to me, students are required to review their drafts with peer tutors in the Writing Center. Below is a sample Book Review Grading Criteria for General Biology I.

TABLE 1. General Biology I Book Review Grading Criteria

TOPICS TO INCLUDE IN THE BOOK REVIEW	POINTS FOR FINAL REPORT
Complete bibliographical reference (at top) using APA or other standard style. No title page. (1 point)	
A total length of approximately two double-spaced pages. (1 point)	
Use of correct spelling, grammar, and sentence structure. (2 points)	
One or two introductory paragraphs consisting of a brief synopsis of the book (in your own words). (4 points)	
Ways in which the book relates to Biology 112 (past or future course topics) (list specific examples). (6 points)	
Major scientific contributions described in the book. How these contribute to your understanding of biology. (4 points)	
How the scientific method was or was not used by the scientists who wrote the book or about whom the book was written. (Describe this in terms of the steps of the scientific method: observations, hypothesis, experiments, and conclusions). (3 points)	
The personal characteristics of the scientist(s) who wrote the book or about whom the book was written. (2 points)	
Personal, physical, political, or professional obstacles the authors or scientist(s) had to overcome. These obstacles should include things such as race, ethnicity, gender, religion, political events, and scientific thought at the time the book was written. (3 points)	
Your personal feelings about the book, the author(s), or the scientist(s) about whom the book was written. Was this book appropriate for a General Biology I student? (4 points)	
TOTAL POINTS OUT OF 30	
Additional comments:	

Chapter 23

Student-Led Teaching Models

Bonnie S. Wood
Biology Department
University of Maine at Presque Isle

Genetics lends itself to teaching with models designed to demonstrate complex processes that occur in the cell itself or are used by laboratory researchers. In my introductory courses I teach with a variety of models described in journals such as *The American Biology Teacher* and *Journal of College Science Teaching.* In my Biology 350 (genetics) course, however, the students themselves assemble and demonstrate models to teach concepts related to course content topics. On the first day of the semester, each student chooses one article from a selection of published papers that describes teaching models for different topics. On the date indicated by the Topic Schedule, a student guides classmates through a complex process by having his or her peers manipulate the components of the model. When preparing their presentations, students are instructed to follow the instructions in the Student-Led Teaching Model Grading Criteria (Table 1, pp. 118–120).

TABLE 1. Student-Led Teaching Model Grading Criteria

(Each listed trait can receive up to 3 points as described below)

Student-presenter's name: _____

Title of article on which model is based: _____

TRAIT	3 POINTS	2 POINTS	1 POINT
ORGANIZATION	Student is well prepared before scheduled class begins and has all materials ready. Student presents sections of teaching model in a logical order, improving upon the sequence suggested by the article to make smoother transitions.	Student completes his/her preparation just before the scheduled class begins. Student follows the exact order suggested by the article.	Student arrives late to class and/or organizes materials at the beginning of the class meeting. Model is presented in an order that is confusing and choppy.
CONTENT	Student reviews background material (often included in introduction of article) and explains how his/her model applies to the week's outline topics and textbook chapter(s). Student uses the model to clarify genetics principles and/or techniques by adding visual and tactile experiences that enhance textbook descriptions.	Student uses the model to demonstrate relevant topics from the week's outline and textbook chapter(s).	Student does not relate the model to relevant topics for the week.
ACCURACY	Student explains all factual material accurately and correctly answers any questions from the instructor or fellow students about the relevant topic. Student is the "class expert" on this topic. Student clearly and correctly defines what each manipulative in the model represents.	Student presents factual material accurately but cannot answer related questions that are beyond the scope of the article. Student uses the manipulatives correctly during the presentation but does not explain what each represents.	Student states factual errors during the presentation and/or incorrectly defines what the manipulatives represent.

(Cont. on p119)

(Cont. from p118)

TRAIT	3 POINTS	2 POINTS	1 POINT
MATERIALS	Student prepares the appropriate amount of materials so that each individual classmate, each pair of classmates, or each learning group has a "kit" with which to work. The amount is determined by being sure that each student has a role and actively participates. Student uses creativity to improve upon or substitute materials suggested by the article or leftover from previous years.	Student provides minimal amount of materials for the class so that some classmates are passive onlookers rather than active participants during the presentation.	Student demonstrates the model but does not engage individual or groups of classmates in manipulating the materials.
PARTICIPATION	Student uses creativity to encourage all classmates to think and learn during the presentation. Student poses at least one question that is different from those suggested by the article.	Student encourages classmates to participate and think, but allows some classmates to be passive and simply listen.	Student demonstrates the model with cookbook-type instructions that do not compel classmates to think.
TEACHING SKILLS	Student speaks confidently and clearly so that all classmates can hear. Student walks around the room to observe and help individuals and groups of classmates manipulate the model and answer questions. Student does not immediately give them answers to questions but instead helps them think through each challenge.	Student gives accurate and clear instructions and waits for classmates to complete each section of the model before proceeding to the next. Student observes individuals and groups as they work on the model.	Student reads instructions directly from article. He/she stands in front of the room and makes little eye contact. Student does not engage in spontaneous teaching with individuals or small groups.

(Cont. on p120)

(Cont. from p. 119)

Section **3**

TRAIT	3 POINTS	2 POINTS	1 POINT
CRITIQUE OF MODEL	During and/or at the end of the presentation, the student highlights strengths and weaknesses of the model and explains how it could be improved to be more accurate. Examples of things the student may describe are: genetics principles the model portrayed accurately; elements that were missing; factual errors that were made in the article; and how the overall model design could have been improved.	At the end of the presentation, student lists strengths and weaknesses of the model.	Student offers no suggestions for improvements or thoughts about the strengths or weaknesses of the model
TOTAL POINTS =			

SECTION 4

General Practices to Improve Assessment

Chapter 24

Eleven Assessment Lessons Learned at the Gate

Mary H. Brown
Lansing Community College
Lansing, Michigan

As a "gateway" instructor for more than 30 years, I've learned a few things about assessing the "typical" community college student. "Gateway" at my institution is the polite euphemism for suggesting you'll always be teaching the nonscience majors with the slim hope that some may eventually learn to tolerate the subject. It's been nearly 20 years since I've evaluated one true science discipline major among the hundreds of students in my classes each academic year. As STEM students are nonexistent in my classes, the best I can hope for is the integrated science major in education.

"Typical community college student" is an oxymoron. There isn't one. Some of my college freshmen are older than I am, returning to college for an opportunity at a retirement career. A few freshmen are dual-enrolled high school students, 16 or 17 years old. Some of my students are parents of young children, and some are grandparents. Today's community college students come from all walks of life and include working adults and recent immigrants or refugees from foreign lands. Included in this mixture is the university's student of choice, whose parents chose the inexpensive route for their first two years of college.

So, how does a "gateway" instructor assess the learning of the "typical" community college student? Included in this chapter are 11 assessment lessons I've learned along the journey.

1. Assessments need to be frequent and scaffolded for legitimate success. Working adults don't want only one or two assessments of their progress during the semester. They want to know exactly how well they are performing in the class at each assignment. They want feedback, personal and directed. These are practical folks! Not surprisingly, they want good grades, but they also want real success. They don't mind being challenged, especially after they've been successful. Successful gateway instructors know that a 16-week semester might have seven or eight large exams. The first exam should be the least challenging. Each subsequent exam should be more challenging. Students want their efforts to show. They want to believe they're progressing, that hard work pays off.

   The experts might suggest that assessments be formative, giving frequent feedback toward the mastery of content. Classroom assessment techniques (CATS) are usually formative assessments, and might include the quick "think pair share" or the "one-minute paper" (Angelo and Cross 1993). Students want definite feedback on all formative assessments. They want to know that you've sincerely read each and every one. Formal grades aren't required, just your attention and constructive remarks in some format.

   Summative assessments are aligned with the evaluation of content mastery or the completion of instruction. Many community college students need state or national benchmarks (standards) for their instruction in their trade or vocational courses. My students see the state and national benchmarks for science education (Roseman and Koppal 2006), and they know that like other professionals, they need to meet those standards. Unlike their certification exams for careers, my class is only the beginning of their journey toward scientific literacy. Benchmarks and standards are a goal for attainment with the expected outcome of lifelong scientific literacy.

2. Assessments and exams are not always the same thing. Assessments come in many forms. In the assessment report I file each year to the divisional office to show that my nonscience majors course is worthy of the title of science "CORE"(which means it meets the criteria of inquiry, shows the processes and limitations of scientific thought, and analyzes data), no fewer than 12 different assessment techniques are listed.

   Assessments include the exams, concept maps (two varieties), Vee diagrams, laboratory reports, and capstone projects. All of these give the instructor information about the students' learning and their mastery of content. Alternative assessments that are real, targeted to the content can be more revealing than an exam. Anxiety plays a role in exam taking, but a student has control over a project. Presentations or projects that allow for research, sharing of ideas, and collaboration are valid assessments. These include contextual, problem-, case-, or performance-based assessments.

3. Embedded assessment across multiple sections has advantages and disadvantages. Community colleges are notorious for having large numbers of adjunct professors. Mine is not an exception. Subsequently, as the full-time professor responsible for reporting on multiple course offerings—even when I am not the "instructor of record"—my job becomes very challenging. Embedded questions on each exam allow for a logistically simple method for tracking all sections of a single course. Instructors simply provide me detail of the embedded questions after each exam. That's the advantage. The disadvantage is that I have no idea why the students miss the embedded questions on particular topics. The variables are too numerous. I have a vague idea within my own classes, as I can monitor absences or recall the day in class when the topic was discussed. There is no information from the classes I didn't teach. The number is a cold sta-

tistic without any qualitative information. After a period of time, the embedded questions on exams must change in their wording. Since the statistical report depends on data from the previous year, altering the question requires a whole set of rationale, without qualitative information. That's another disadvantage.

4. Listening provides more assessment value than talking. As my students engage in their laboratory activities, I listen. I listen to their interactions, collaborations, and arguments. I walk to each lab table, and I listen. I can learn a tremendous amount about their learning and their assimilation of the content by listening. During the course of the semester, they become very accustomed to me walking to each table without saying anything as they work. I learn a lot about their thinking processes by listening. Each unit of instruction also begins with me listening. Each collaborative group is asked to list prior knowledge about topics in the unit. Together we summarize. We use the prior knowledge expressed in discussions to increase the depth of knowledge on the topics. Pre-assessment starts with listening.

Each unit of the courses I teach starts with a series of connection questions. What do you already know about the topic? How can learning this information be useful to you? What are you looking forward to learning about this topic? Each unit also ends with reflection. What did you learn about this topic? Did anything you learned in this unit change your mind? How will this information be useful for your future? Postassessment also starts with listening. I've learned that students do not necessarily answer these questions unless they are explicitly asked. If there exists a possibility that you could be called upon and expected to respond directly to a specific question, you prepare a response. Without that potential accountability, it's a rare student who prepares a response or who is introspective without the prompting questions.

5. A wrong answer has tremendous value. A well-thought-out, detailed wrong answer gives you lots of information. It provides you opportunity to correct a misconception or to craft a discrepant event to allow the learner to construct a more scientifically accurate response. Providing the question in advance and allowing two minutes to think before calling on a student to respond yields more information than simply calling on a student. Wait time also works well (Rowe 2003). Giving students a 30-second warning before expecting a response is very powerful. "I'm going to ask <student's name> to respond to the next question" gives that individual a few extra seconds to compose an answer. The responses are more complete, even when they are wrong.

6. Assessment need to be clearly tied to outcomes, objectives, or learning targets. Both instructor and student need to clearly know the purpose of the assessment. What are we evaluating? Communications of expectations are important. Providing the format of the exam gives students an opportunity to prepare appropriately. You study differently for a written essay than a multiple-choice exam. You prepare differently for a presentation than for a discussion.

7. Assessments that are viewed as "products" by students are sources of pride. I have many "product" assessments in my classes. I'm always surprised by college students who have told me that their perfect score concept map was hung on their refrigerator! Or the lab report with the phrase "Well done!" was read over the dinner table. It seems it doesn't really matter how old we are, a well-done product is a source of pride. Community college students know the rewards of hard work. They work tremendously hard in the challenges of everyday life. They can do exceptional work when the assessment is viewed as a product.

8. Detailed constructive feedback on assessments is essential. It takes about six hours to correct a stack of 24 lab reports, if they are well writ-

Section

4

ten. A set of poorly written lab reports takes about twice as long. Each report needs carefully worded constructive feedback. Rubrics on written assignments (and oral for presentations) are given in advance, and students are expected to follow the same criteria for excellence in writing as they would in a composition class. Even on exams, common mistakes are explained. The feedback on the exam is another opportunity to teach.

9. Owning and expressing your expectations for their success is crucial. Students rise to the challenge of high expectations. When given rationale for a challenge, they accept. They will even accept the frustrations of disequilibrium if they understand the rationale. Explicit reasons for content expectations are essential. Community college students will accept the "because it's on the test" but are likely to ask you why it's on the test. They want a more practical reason for learning the content. Ideally, the reason is tied to a potential career, or an everyday application.

10. Assessments need to be varied, perceived as fair and attainable, and evaluated both objectively and subjectively (Mintzes, Wandersee, and Novak, 1999). The brain loves novelty. It fatigues when offered routine. With 12 different types of assessments throughout the semester, fatigue is more physical than cerebral! Each exam has a variety of question types. Students create or correct concept maps; they evaluate true and false statements, correcting the false. They also write brief answers and traditional multiple paragraph essays. Each exam also has multiple-choice questions and paragraph completions. Students analyze their exam results at the conclusion of each unit and write goals to improve weak performance areas. Students know how exams are evaluated. They know that each section is evaluated independently without my knowledge of the test author. They also know when the sections of the exam are totaled, I often write encour-

aging remarks on their progress (e.g., "Nice improvement on this multiple-choice section; keep working!") Statistical analysis is given on the entire class performance, and the class discusses improvement strategies for the next exam. Besides the exams, alternative assessments are a near daily occurrence.

11. Ideally, assessments inform teaching, and self-assessments can even inform the learner. Assessment is *not* only about evaluating the learning process. It should change the teaching process. Each assessment should inform the instructor as to needed changes in pedagogy, presentation or missing fundamentals for conceptual understanding. Self-assessments can provide the learner with great potential to change.

The view from the "gate" as I encourage students to consider the science disciplines is generally positive. Together, the students and I investigate, listen to each other, and plan our journey together. Although assessment reports are needed for multiple levels (divisional, program, departmental) there is enough consistency across the requirements that only the perspective changes. Not only have I learned how to assess my "typical" community college students so that I know what they are learning, I've also learned how to teach better science through our shared assessments.

References

Angelo, T. A., and K. P. Cross. 1993. *Classroom assessment technique: A handbook for college teachers.* 2nd ed. San Francisco, CA: Jossey Bass Publishers.

Mintzes, J., J. Wandersee, and J. Novak, eds. 1999. *Assessing science understanding: A human constructivist view.* San Francisco, CA: Academic Press.

Roseman, J. E., and M. Koppal. 2006. Ensuring that college graduates are science literate:

Implications of K-12 benchmarks and standards. In *Handbook of College Science Teaching*, eds. J. Mintzes, and J. Leonard, 325–349. Arlington, VA: NSTA Press.

Rowe, M. 2003. Wait-time and rewards as instructional variables, their influence on language, logic, and fate control: Part one—wait-time. *Journal of Research in Science Teaching.* Vol. S1, 19–32.

Chapter 25

Developing Assessment Performance Indicators

Peter Kandlbinder
Institute for Interactive Media and Learning,
University of Technology, Sydney
Sydney, Australia

Introduction

The goal of assessment is to judge how well a student has learned. This information has a range of uses but is mainly used to improve student learning or for the accreditation of student performance. These two purposes alone make assessment one of the most important aspects of university teaching (Brown, Bull, and Pendlebury 1997; Gibbs 1992; Ramsden 2003). In the process of assessing students, clear messages are sent about what is valued in a course. Recognition that assessment represents the de facto curriculum (Rowntree 1987) is usually followed by the observation that lecturers can use these effects to influence student learning. In short, if an assessment scheme can be interpreted by students, then we need to ensure that the messages sent match with what lecturer's value.

Finding the balance between what is commonly referred to as the "backwash effect" (see for example Watkins, Dahli, and Ekholm 2005) to promote student learning and teaching activities is what Biggs (2003) calls "constructive alignment." This chapter is a first attempt to develop a valid method for lecturers to determine the balance their subject has achieved between its learning outcome and its chosen assessment tasks. By recognizing that the characteristics of the different assessment items influence students' perceptions of their study, it is proposed that it is possible

Section

4

to rate the effectiveness of the arrangement of assessment items for student learning. The purpose of providing different weightings for an assessment pattern would be to encourage academic staff to favor particular assessment tasks in relation to student workload and feedback that have been shown to encourage students to adopt deep approaches to learning.

Assessment's Impact on Student Experience

A review of the assessment literature suggests that the overall pattern of assessment items can provide an effective means of judging the alignment and balance of an assessment scheme. It has long been recognized that different assignment formats influence students' approaches to their study. Students who perceive that the assessment will test memorization are more likely to adopt a surface approach to learning (Scouller 1998). Lecturers, therefore, elect to use a range of assessment tasks to ensure a balance between coverage and depth of understanding. Biggs (2003) argues that validity is achieved when the assessment items assess the kind of knowledge desired in particular content areas. Assessment tasks vary in the type of achievement they target. For example, timed examinations focus on memorization over a broad range of topics (Piper, Nulty, and O'Grady 1996). Essays can measure understanding, synthesis, and evaluation skills but do so in depth rather than across a range of topics (Brown, Bull, and Pendlebury 1997).

It can be difficult for lecturers to locate advice on how to create an assessment pattern to achieve these goals. Explanations of assessment go into great detail about individual characteristics of assessments without describing how each of the pieces fit into the whole. Numerous checklists document the different methods and strategies available for assessment without calculating the relative merit of different selections and instruments necessary for achieving the course goals. For example, a recent survey of assessment

practices (James, McInnis, and Devlin 2002) developed 16 indicators of effective assessment in higher education. It represents the characteristics of good assessment but provides no indication of how a lecturer is to use the checklist to change educational practice.

To become an effective assessor Stiggins (1993) suggests that teachers need a clear image of what should be attained by the students, an understanding of the range of alternatives to assess the targeted attainments and to understand how all of the various aspects translate into assessment tasks. In order to change their assessment pattern, lecturers need practical procedural steps that they can be confident will promote sound assessment practices. Descriptions of different ways to assess students simply have no way of expressing the relative value of decisions made by academics. As a result, students continue to complain of being over-assessed, and academics feel burdened by marking but do not know what needs to be changed to promote sound assessment of student learning.

Judging the Assessment Pattern

When deciding how to assess student learning, there are a range of factors that need to be considered. What can be judged through the assessment pattern is the combination of assessment items and their scheduling over the semester. In determining this combination, lecturers have to decide on not only the goals of the assessment task but the type of assessment, how it relates to other assessment items in the semester, its weighting, who will do the marking, and the type of feedback students will receive. Before describing a framework for how these premises interact, I will briefly describe some of the critical parameters needed in judging the appropriate balance in an assessment pattern in a little more detail.

Most assessment types exhibit features distinctive from those in other categories. Class presentations, for example, have a performative element that is missing from essays or reports. Within the broad spectrum of assessment types it is therefore worthwhile to make the distinction between an assessment item's primary and secondary purposes. For each of the assessment types, it is possible to distinguish between what an assessment task is particularly good at or can do uniquely well. An assessment type could be primary in the sense of being the only one able to address certain assessment goals, but secondary in other areas of knowledge or skill. Freeman and Lewis (1999) provide a good overview of the strengths and weaknesses of various assessment types and their review suggests that essays might be primarily used to determine the logic of a student's argument but only secondarily used to determine the declarative knowledge used as evidence for that argument. Multiple-choice questions, on the other hand, are particularly good at testing declarative knowledge but poor at determining student reasoning.

While the assessment type affects which of the students' abilities are sampled, assessment for learning relies primarily on formative feedback that tells students how to improve their work. Feedback is any discussion of the difference between a desired and an actual result designed to support student learning. The quality of feedback is often mentioned by students as the most significant factor in their learning (Kandlbinder 2002). For feedback to be effective, students must be able to apply the comments they receive to improve their chances of success with the following assignment. These comments can take the form of grades, checklists, or in-class comments, with the simplest being a check or grade and the most valuable to students being detailed, individualized written comments. High levels of feedback result in high-quality student outcomes by aligning the results of the students' work more closely to expectations of the course. In the case of feedback, comparability between students is far less important than the immediacy of the feedback (Gibbs and Simpson 2005).

The frequency and duration of assignments affect the assessment pattern's reliability and the ability of lecturers to provide feedback on student progress. Less frequent assessment means that the greater proportion of the student's final mark rests on each assignment. A single assignment worth 100% of the student's final marks results in a highly concentrated and correspondingly stressful period of student and lecturer activity. As a general principle, reliability in assessment can be achieved by setting more but shorter assessment items and using more than one assessor (Brown and Knight 1998). The greater number of assessment tasks spreads the risk of the students doing uncharacteristically poorly, and there will be a higher consistency in the students' results. Students will also receive more guidance on their performance through constructive feedback, resulting in less anxiety and fewer demands on lecturers to explain what is required.

Although a greater number of assessment items brings with it greater reliability, Brown and Knight (1998) caution that reliability in assessment comes at a cost of validity. Smaller, discrete tasks are less authentic than large, ill-defined problems that imitate the kinds of tasks students are likely to experience when they graduate. Aspects of the curriculum that are sampled become narrower, and there is less contact between the tutor and student, with a resulting decline of student motivation as they work only to meet deadlines (Gibbs 1992). Further, feedback becomes more impersonal, and consequently students also produce work of poorer quality outside of what could normally be expected.

Integrating Assessment Items Into an Assessment Pattern

The difficulty with identifying such an array of different variables is in understanding how these indicators can be combined into a meaningful whole. What is required to make sense of the range of variables is a procedure for choosing an appropriate course of action, at the same time

Section

4

being mindful that the choice does not generate dysfunctional consequences. While assessment should not unduly favor one student over another, research has confirmed that there is a wide level of agreement that the goal of higher education is for students to adopt a deep approach to their learning (see Ramsden 2003 for details). The assessment pattern therefore needs to ensure that it consists of the appropriate balance of assessment tasks that provide the greatest chance of students achieving these high-quality learning outcomes.

To determine which factors were related to the students' responses to assessment, the results of the 2002 University of Technology, Sydney Course Experience Questionnaire (n = 2998) were statistically analyzed. Hierarchical regression analysis revealed that student workload (from Appropriate Workload Scale) and teacher feedback (from Good Teaching Scale) were important predictors of students' perceptions of assessment (from Appropriate Assessment Scale). Student workload and teacher feedback

yielded beta weights of 0.23 (p<0.01), and 0.15 (p<0.01) respectively. Further, goal alignment (from the Clear Goals and Standards Scale) was found to interact significantly and positively with teacher feedback (beta weight = 0.05, p<0.05). These associations formed the basis of a general model, incorporating the different aspects of assessment that influence students' perceptions and lead to high quality learning outcomes, as shown in Figure 1.

A Simple Tool to Evaluate an Assessment Pattern

Having drawn up a list of factors and variables that impact the students' perceptions of assessment, the next task is to convert this model into a simple tool that can be used by academic staff to make decisions about assessment patterns. This conversion requires a number of assumptions to be made that will simplify the

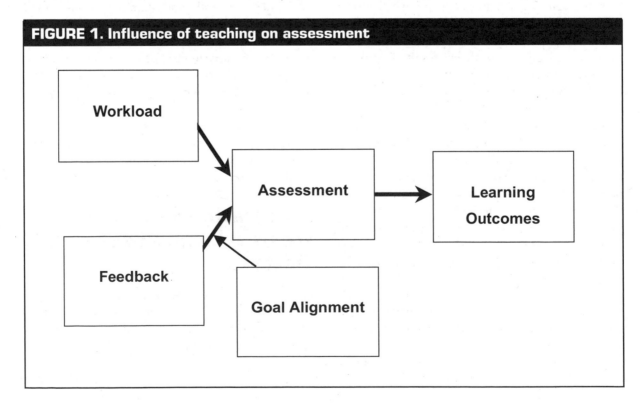

FIGURE 1. Influence of teaching on assessment

problem of putting together all of the factors influencing assessment. It needs to be made clear at this stage that the model in Figure 1 is only useful for evaluating an existing assessment pattern, not for creating a single ideal assessment scheme. It is up to individual lecturers to determine what assessment tasks will be used and how they will be combined. Lecturers, however, can be steered toward using certain desirable assessment practices by making explicit the assumptions that lie behind the assessment model.

For example, at present there is an almost universal reliance on three assessment tasks for a typical higher education subject: class presentation, essay, and examination. Yet, university teaching is presented as promoting broad generic skills, like problem solving and critical thinking, which may be more effectively assessed with other, more holistic methods, such as projects and portfolios. Therefore, it would be desirable to encourage academics to adopt assessment tasks that evaluate a range of different abilities, such as the use of portfolios to capture the complexity of meaningful real-life tasks. This, of course, needs to be balanced by the lecturer's understanding of what is practical given the limitations of the course, such as the number of students involved.

As a result of these combinations of course goals, feedback, and student workload, it is possible to derive numeric outcomes for assessment performance that can be plotted over the course of the semester. Optimal values can be determined for the spacing of the assignments, type of markers, and style of feedback for each assessment type. A calculation of the overall quality of the assessment pattern is then a case of entering values that represent the current assessment pattern which can then be compared with the optimum value determined for each assessment task. The overall pattern could, as a final comparison, be averaged and the means compared to departmentally determined norms.

For example, let us assume that in higher education the optimum balance between adequate feedback and moderate student workload appears to be somewhere between three and five assessment items. This number is derived from the principle that students are able to take deeper approaches to the learning if the number of assessable tasks is small. The assessment tasks, however, need to be well spaced over the semester to allow students sufficient time to complete each task, and the teacher sufficient time to contribute the relevant feedback on their learning. If the same three tasks are each due in the final week of semester, they do not achieve the same degree of balanced student workload, as there is no opportunity for students to receive formative feedback.

To calculate the relative values of this assessment pattern requires firstly calculating the number of weeks since the previous assignment. This has been placed in a row labelled "Weeks since previous assignment" in Table 1 (p. 134). In this example it has been assumed that an essay requires five weeks to complete, a report requires four weeks, a class presentation three weeks, and multiple-choice and short-answer questions only one week. Each of these values is ascribed as the denominator in the appropriate table cell. In comparing the actual time with the ideal assessment timing, any assessment decision that sets an assessment task at a value less than the attributed level will, in the case of student workload, be considered to exceed workload expectations by not allocating sufficient time to complete the work. In a similar manner a value is derived for the marker (in the example below, 1 for lecturer, 2 for self, and 3 for peer marker) and style of feedback. For the sake of this example, feedback has been assigned a value of 1 for a mark only, 2 for mark with comment, 3 for use of a checklist, 4 for verbal comments in class, and 5 for detailed written comments. Each of the actual values would be derived from departmental expectations and deliberation on what practices the department would like to encourage, such as detailed written feedback in essays.

Section

4

TABLE 1. Measuring the assessment pattern					
Type of assessment tasks	Essay	Report	Class presentation	Multiple-choice quiz	Short answer question
Weeks since previous assignment	2 / 5	/ 4	5 / 3	5 / 1	/ 1
Marker	1 / 2	/ 2	1 / 1	1 / 1	/ 1
Formative feedback	2 / 5	/ 2	2 / 4	1 / 2	/ 3
Total	1.3		3.1	6.5	

To compare an assessment pattern, the sum of each column is compared with its idealized total of 3. The average of all assessment tasks can also be compared to a departmental norm. Table 1 above represents an assessment pattern of a multiple-choice quiz in Week 5 followed by a class presentation in Week 10 and an essay in Week 12. All assignments are marked by the lecturer and, with the exception of the multiple-choice questions, are given a grade with a comment. In this example the multiple-choice questions and the essay are the furthest from idealized assessment pattern scoring 6.5 and 1.3 respectively. A classroom presentation five weeks after the multiple-choice quiz is about what would be expected (3.1). Simply swapping the timing of the essay and multiple-choice questions would bring each closer to its normative expectation for both individual assignments and the average for the assessment pattern overall (2.8 compared to 3.6).

Changing Assessment Patterns

Aside from the inarguable benefits of validity and reliability, the question of procedural fairness in assessment is rarely explicitly addressed. Fairness stems from the conditions that ensure that all students have an equal opportunity to achieve to the best of their ability. The likely consequences on student learning should therefore be considered whenever assessments are planned. Students adopt a deep approach for learning when their goal is to understand ideas and seek meaning by relating new things to things they already know. Prosser and Trigwell (1999) argue that students who adopted a deep approach to learning have the highest quality learning outcomes and report greater student satisfaction than either surface or disintegrating approaches to learning.

Rational decision making would suggest that all academics are aiming for the assessment pattern that is most likely to encourage the highest quality learning in students. The ideal assessment pattern would only use assessments that add to the student having the greatest opportunity to adopt a deep approach to learning. When it comes to interpreting the principles of assessment for academic practice, however, there is no point of comparison from which to know whether a change is for the better. Without practical guidance many attempts to improve assessment involve simply accepting the current practices (Rowntree 1987).

To conclude, I have argued in this chapter that there needs to be a normative as well as a descriptive measure of the design of assessment patterns so that educators can compare themselves against the ideals to which they can aspire. Academics have considerable autonomy in choosing their assessment items, though individual lecturers tend not to give too much thought to changing assessment. Many lecturers would be unaware of how the different aspects of assessment can be combined to improve the quality of student learning. By weighting the key principles of assessment to reflect the goals of universities and its programs, targeting multiple achievements and ensuring fitness for purpose, a calculation of assessment performance indicators can produce useful and informative data for academics to determine how well their assessment patterns meet the criterion of effective assessment.

Acknowledgment

I wish to thank Adam Morgan for carrying out the statistical analysis of the Course Experience Questionnaire data.

References

Biggs, J. B. 2003. *Teaching for quality learning at university: What the student does.* 2nd ed. Buckingham, UK: Society for Research into Higher Education & Open University Press.

Brown, G., J. Bull, and M. Pendlebury. 1997. *Assessing student learning in higher education.* London, UK: Routledge.

Brown, S., and P. Knight. 1998. *Assessing learners in higher education.* London, UK: Kogan Page.

Freeman, R., and R. Lewis. 1999. *Planning and implementing assessment.* London, UK: Kogan Page.

Gibbs, G. 1992. *Assessing more students.* Oxford, UK: Oxford Centre for Staff Development.

Gibbs, G. and C. Simpson. 2005. Conditions under which assessment supports students' learning. *Learning and Teaching in Higher Education* 1: 3–31.

James, R., C. McInnis, and M. Devlin. 2002. *Assessing learning in Australian universities.* Melbourne: Centre for the Study of Higher Education.

Kandlbinder, P. 2002. *Connecting with students through formative feedback.* Paper presented at the Closing the Loop: Evaluations and Assessment Conference, Brisbane, Australia.

Piper, D. W., D. Nulty, and G. O'Grady. 1996. *Examination practices and procedures in Australian universities* (No. 0644472464). Canberra: Australian Government Publication Service.

Prosser, M., and K. Trigwell. 1999. *Understanding learning and teaching: The experience in higher education.* Buckingham: SRHE & Open University Press.

Ramsden, P. 2003. *Learning to teach in higher education.* 2nd ed. London, UK: Routledge Falmer.

Rowntree, D. 1987. *Assessing students: How shall we know them?* 2nd ed. London: Kogan Page.

Scouller, K. 1998. The influence of assessment method on students' learning approaches: Multiple choice question examination vs. essay assignment. *Higher Education* 35 (4): 453–472.

Stiggins, R. J. 1993. Teacher training in assessment: Overcoming the neglect. In *Teacher training in measurement and assessment skills*, ed. S. L. Wise. Lincoln, NE: Buros Institute of Mental Measurements.

Watkins, D., B. Dahli, and M. Ekholm. 2005. Awareness of the backwash effect of assessment: A phenomenographic study of the views of Hong Kong and Swedish lecturers. *Instructional Science* 33 (4): 283–309.

Chapter 26

Practices That Jeopardize Bona Fide Student Assessment

Thomas R. Lord
Department of Biology
Indiana University of Pennsylvania
Indiana, Pennsylvania

Most authorities agree that student assessment plays a major role in successful instruction at all levels of education. Student assessment is the means by which teachers, the directors of the learning experience, appraise the success of their lessons on students, the product of the instruction. Teachers at every level of instruction realize the importance of fair, reliable, and valid assessment. They also understand the outcomes riding on the accuracy of the evaluations and that mismanagement carries such consequences as jeopardizing student futures, course integrity, and the reputation of the institution.

To meet the challenges, educational theorists have created dozens of design plans and rubrics to help instructors accurately assess the members of their classes. However, there are nearly as many evaluation practices that have developed that discredit and sometimes nullify honest assessment attempts as there are dependable practices. This chapter addresses the question of what types of assessment are detrimental and invalidate attempts for true and meaningful student assessment.

Reliable assessment is threatened when tests are poorly constructed.

Evaluation based on testing is the most prevalent means of student assessment. However, few college professors have had instruction on meaningful test development, and therefore, it is common for them to resort to test items based on content recall. Most items provided on the test banks supplied by the publisher of the text used in the course tend to fall into this category. These questions are the simplest to create and the easiest to grade. On the thinking hierarchy developed by Benjamin Bloom in 1956, content recall is placed in the lowest category, and studies on the topic have found that 75% of the test items developed for undergraduate college students fall within this category (Huint 2004; Lord and Blaviskar 2007). So predictable is the use of low-level thinking questions on tests that students don't attempt to develop higher-order thinking skills such as analysis, synthesis, and evaluation. Not only does term recall simplify what a student studies, it discourages students from relating what they are learning to more complicated associated ideas. Why should students work hard during their busy daily routines to develop higher-order thinking skills when the exams used to evaluate their understanding are at the lowest level of Bloom's Taxonomy? This idea is strongly supported by studies that show that, indeed, low-level learning severely dampens enthusiasm for understanding at higher levels (Bransford, Brown, and Cocking 2002).

Reliable assessment is threatened when collusion occurs among members in the class.

Research has found that course instructors must provide a clear policy for what happens if students cheat (Hinman 2004). There are many important things instructors can do from this perspective, such as discussing what constitutes cheating, and the importance of academic honesty, putting an honor code in place, explaining what measures will be in place to prevent and detect cheating, and describing the punishments for cheating. If students perceive that the instructor does not care about cheating, then incidents of both spontaneous and planned cheating increase (Cizek 2003). Students quickly realize when cheaters are seldom caught and the punishment isn't harsh for those who do. Kleinger (2000) found that punishment for cheating is one of the main deterrents to student collusion.

Reliable assessment is threatened when question format on lengthy exams is not varied.

Several studies have found that it is important to vary the type of questions students are expected to answer in lengthy objective exams. Students become fatigued over long, test-taking episodes, and it has been found that pupil success rises when exams contain a variety of different question styles that include multiple-choice, short-answer, and essay questions (Breedlove, Burkett, and Winfield 2004).

Reliable assessment is threatened when only a single version of the exam is used in large group testing situations.

When exams are administered to large populations of students who are sitting close to one another in a lecture theater, the temptation is great for class members to compare their responses with that of neighboring students. It is important, therefore, that professors draw questions from a large bank of items and distribute different versions of the exam to test takers in the hall (Cizek 2003).

Reliable assessment is threatened when different versions of the exam have their questions varied in chunked groups rather then scrambled on the test.

Cizek (2003) discovered that students can quickly find test questions when they are blocked together but have a very difficult time locating analogous test items when they are scrambled throughout the exam. In fact, a study of students' perceived effectiveness of cheating prevention strategies conducted by Cizek found that having scrambled test forms was the number one factor for the prevention of cheating.

Reliable assessment is threatened when lengthy exams are utilized to determine grades.

Studies have found that a more accurate measure of student knowledge occurs when shorter tests, rather than longer ones are used to assess students. The researchers found shorter tests reduce the incentive to cheat, as each test isn't as likely to make or break a student's grade; the pressure of a single midterm and final creates a strong incentive to cheat on those exams (Strauss and Spreen 1998).

Reliable assessment is threatened when online course grades are blended with in-class grades.

College courses are being offered online more than ever before. The distance aspects of the courses, however, create new and interesting questions on the integrity of assessment instruments. Despite innovative practices being developed to help alleviate the concern, major problems still exist, especially when assessment is based on subjective exams taken by students from their homes (Kruger and Dunning 1999).

Reliable assessment is threatened when exams are not proctored by the instructor or a designate.

With proctored exams, instructors feel more in control of the testing environment and more able to combat cheating in a familiar classroom setting. In a study on cheating in math or fact-based courses, Trenholm (2007) concluded that proctoring is the single greatest tool colleges presently have to uphold the integrity of the educational process in instruction in science, math, or fact-based courses.

Reliable assessment is threatened when the same exam is given to students each semester.

College instructors should realize that, sooner or later, copies of exam questions they permit class members to keep will quickly become distributed to future students. Annual changes to the test bank for each unit will minimize the impact this has on the integrity of assessment. Researchers have found that even minor changes such as re-wording the questions and changing the order of answers can help extend the useful life of a test bank (McChesney 2007).

Reliable assessment is threatened when student grades are based only on tests.

Science is full of information gleaned outside of the tests. Many courses include meaning-ful out-of-class assignments that students can do. Reports on experiments, graphic data, lo-cal surveys, collections, and preservations are all examples. Science disciplines are full of is-sues that student teams can research, debate, present, or write reports on (cloning, xeno-transplants, stem cells, Hubble discoveries, nuclear energy/weapons, chemical warfare, evolution/creation, drug safety). Students can select a special project or work on a team proj-ect that would be completed at semester's end. Examples include local water/soils/vegetation analysis, simple machine inventions, local stream chemistry, or herbal garden design. Outside reading or reports can be selected on topical science issues (e.g., *Gorillas in the Mist, Fingerprints of the Gods, Nature and Destiny of Man*) and classical science literature (e.g., *Double Helix, Silent Spring, Origin of Species*). Research or reports can be done on a luminary such as Pasteur, Newton, or Darwin. Any activity that involves students in more than just attending class develops attitudes and understandings and should be recognized and counted in the student's assessment. It not only helps students who have test phobias but also develops a more complete understanding of what science is all about (Rutherford 1999).

Reliable assessment is threatened when numerous corrections and inaccuracies appear on the exam.

It's not uncommon during the initial part of their test periods for professors to spend time correcting a plethora of spelling, grammar, punctuation, and chart errors. Studies indicate anxieties in students rise rapidly when correc-tion time is taken at the test's onset, and as the uneasiness rises, the test taker has more dif-ficulty thinking logically about the questions. Realizing that correction time is detrimental to learning, it's suggested that instructors make every attempt to correct errors on the exam before copies of it are generated (Dodd et al. 1990).

Reliable assessment is threatened when test questions and items are disorganized or sloppily presented.

Anxiety also rises in students when the test is dif-ficult to follow, either because of its wording or its shabby appearance. It is not uncommon, for example, for charts, diagrams, and other graph-ics from poor-quality sources to be pasted onto exams or for handwritten phrases that are diffi-cult to decipher to be added. For a valid evalua-tion of student understanding to occur, students need to receive exams that are neat and accurate (Matsuda 1993).

Reliable assessment is threatened when nomenclature and vocabulary used in the exam is at a significantly higher level than the vocabulary used during presentation times.

Research has found test anxiety rises quickly when the wording on the test differs significantly from the words and phrases used during the lessons. This is particularly true when questions on the exam are drawn from a variety of alternate sources, such as a test bank from a different publisher or from ancient copies of the test. Students should be given the chance to experience the thoroughness of the nomenclature they're expected to know before the day the test is given (Johnson 2006).

Reliable assessment is threatened when students are given credit for simply attending class.

Often instructors give credit to students for just attending class, a practice that should be expected and not rewarded. Some professors feel that students learn from hearing information mentioned during the class period, reading material before class or turning in assignments. "Perhaps the students aren't studying outside of class," state Sleigh and Ritzer (2001), "but at least they've seen the examples, slides, or transparencies and heard the nomenclature." The research finds, however, that students do not learn by being present in the class. "To learn, the brain must be ready to accept and transmit information. Students should not be rewarded simply because they come to class" (Caine 2005).

Reliable assessment is threatened when students come to class but aren't attentive.

Contemporary research finds that couch-potato students rarely energize their brains enough to remember information for very long (Lord 2002). Students need to be involved in the learning process, an action frequently spoken of as "hands-on, minds-on teaching" (Gelula 2004). Students in classes dominated by the instructor do not recall information for more than a few weeks without the professor's constant reinforcement (Cross and Angelo 1988). Accurate assessment of students, instructors, and courses is seriously jeopardized when students don't pay attention to what's going on in class.

Reliable assessment is threatened when instructors grade tests on a curve.

In this day and age, most students expect the professor to curve grades if the overall majority of the scores on an exam fall below the acceptable average score. Students' poor performances on an exam may indeed suggest that the instruction was poor or that the questions asked on the test were above the level of the instruction. However, if the examination was constructed to challenge student thinking and fairly represents the teaching of the material, the students shouldn't be given higher point values than they deserve. Most academics agree that it is not positive to shift student averages, lowering score cutoffs, to give them better grades, but they resort to it to pass more class members. Such practice only legitimizes a student's laziness and irresponsibility and reinforces an attitude of not being challenged in work. Good courses lose their integrity when teachers reward students with points they haven't earned. If scores are low and the professor feels something must be done to rectify the situation, he or she can ask the students to retake another exam or complete meaningful work similar to the material missed on the exam. Students should work for their grades, not simply be given them (Hunter 2006).

Reliable assessment is threatened when credit is given for real-life experiences.

Students sometimes ask to have a test waived or course credit given for life experiences they've had. It's sometimes possible, for example, for students to get credit for a science course if they worked for an agency related to the course subject. A student who spent a summer internship with a biological or chemical industry, for example, might seek to wave a course requirement related to their intern experience.

The assumption is that the practical experience gained from such an event far outweighs what a student would learn in the course. While this may be true in some situations, there are practical experiences presented by students that are not as valuable as being in the course. In addition, the student has presumbly already received credit in some form for the practical experience and shouldn't be able to receive additional credit for the same experience for a second course (Kruger and Dunning 1999).

Reliable assessment is threatened when outside variables are not controlled in student work.

While well-designed independent study is an educationally valuable way to receive academic credit, there are sometimes serious flaws in the design of the initiative that jeopardize the accuracy of the outcomes. An example of this would be projects in which variables are poorly controlled in the investigation. This occurred recently when a student wished to test the hypothesis that taking vitamin C over the winter increases the resistance to cold and flu germs. Starting at the first of the year, the originator of the proposal took a 5 mg tablet of vitamin C each day of the winter semester. Over that time she recorded in a diary all cold or flu episodes she experienced (sluggishness, runny nose). At the end of the semester, she had recorded only a half-dozen lethargic days and concluded her hypothesis was correct: that vitamin C was a suitable defense against colds and flu. She received an A for her independent work. The student, however, should not have gotten credit for such a poorly designed experiment. Variables were not constrained and a control group was not utilized. Additionally, the researcher should not have been the subject in the study (Gibson 1961).

Reliable assessment is threatened when surrogate situations are substituted for real outcomes in student projects.

Students sometime propose projects that embrace surrogate comparisons. Such "if..., then" analogies, however, are sometimes not equivalent and make the analogy untrue. For example, a student begins a research project on the effect vitamin B12 has on the growth of Chlamydomonas, a single cell green algae but halfway through has trouble obtaining the unicellular algae. At this point the researching student decides to substitute another chlorophyll-rich single cell algae (e.g., Chlorella) for the original and continues his or her experiment with the surrogate. The logic is that vitamin B12 has the same effect on Chlorella as it had on Chlamydomonas. This is another example of not understanding what research is all about. Documentation needs to be presented to verify this assumption if it is to be accepted and the student is to be awarded credit for the project (Korn, Albert, and McShane 2005).

Reliable assessment is threatened when personal clashes occur between the instructor and student(s).

Grades awarded for a course should not be influenced by opinion differences between the professor and one or more of the students in the class. A few years ago one of my graduate advisees had a personal problem with a professor, which resulted in a failing grade in the course. When the grade was challenged and the situation was investigated, the college sided with its employee. The grade remained on the student's record and she was dismissed from the graduate program. With the blemish on her transcript, she has not been able to gain admission to another graduate school and now works at a local grocery store.

Reliable assessment is threatened when professors romantically interact with one or more students.

Platonic, professional, interpersonal, and emotional encounters sometimes develop during a student's academic career. Assessment can be deeply influenced by a relationship beyond innocent friendship. Many colleges and universities have instituted policies against such developments but the rights of consenting adults may challenge these rules. If this situation is likely to occur, efforts should be taken to move the student to another professor's section of the course (Chervin 2000).

Reliable assessment is threatened when lesson information is too advanced for the students to understand.

Students sometimes select courses that fit their schedules rather than courses they've met through prerequisites. When students are unprepared for a course, they usually lose interest in the instruction and stop preparing for the class. Disinterested students also tend to develop negative attitudes toward the course and dislike for the professor. It is, therefore, important that proper advisement take place and prerequisites are followed before students schedule their classes (Tamir, Welch, and Rakow 1995; Bontempo 2005).

Reliable assessment is threatened when lesson information is only anecdotal rather than factual.

Occasionally, when instructors attempt to clarify points they've made, they resort to oversimplified, insubstantial, or nonverifiable terminology in an effort to aid comprehension. Rather than helping understanding, however, the simplification often causes more confusion than it alleviates. For example, in trying to explain the way a snake moves, the instructor created a series of waves along a length of rope. This raised more questions than it settled and realizing this, the instructor withdrew the analogy. In an effort to simplify the event, the professor created more of a problem (Fiorello 2001).

Accurate, bona fide student assessment is essential if colleges and universities are to maintain their respected reputations. Due to the profound consequences, the task of maintaining accurate assessment is constantly under scrutiny by stakeholders at the institutions. If academics do not devote their efforts and resources to maintaining their value and quality, the integrity and future existence of their institutio--n is jeopardized.

References

Bilgrami, A., J. Cole and J. Elster. 2005. The clash of ideas at Columbia. *New York Times* April 11.

Bloom, B., M. Englehart, E. Furst, W. Hill, and D. Krathwohl. 1956. *Taxonomy of educational objectives: The classification of educational goals.* New York: McKay.

Bontempo, B. 2005. Will to learn. *Education,* Summer.

Bransford, J. D., A. L. Brown, and R. R. Cocking. 2002. *How people learn: Brain, mind, experience and school.* Washington, DC: National Academy Press.

Breedlove, B., T. Burkett, and I. Winfield. 2004. Collaborative testing and test performance. *Academic Exchange Quarterly* 8 (3).

Caine, R. N. 2005. *Brain/mind learning principles in action.* Thousand Oaks, CA: Corwin Press.

Chervin, R. 2000. Idol worship of the "A" and the student/professor relationship. *University Concourse* 5 (7): 3–4.

Cizek, G. J. 2003. *Detecting and preventing classroom cheating: Promoting integrity in assessment.* Thousand Oaks, CA: Corwin Press.

Cross, P., and T. Angelo. 1988. *Classroom assessment techniques: A handbook for faculty.* Technical Report No 88-A-004.0. Ann Arbor, Michigan: National Center for Research to Improving Post Secondary Teaching and Learning.

Dodd, J. M., M. Hermanson, J. R. Nelson, and J. Fischer. 1990. Tribal college faculty willingness to provide accommodations to students with learning disabilities. *Journal of American Indian Education* 30 (1).

Fiorello, C. A. 2001. Common myths of children's behavior. *Skeptical Inquirer* 25 (3): 37–39.

Gelula, R. 2004. *Survey on sleep in America.* Washington, DC: National Science Foundation Press.

Gibson, W. A. 1961. Extending latent class solutions to other variables. *Psychometrika* New York: Springer Publishing.

Guest, K., and D. Murphy. 2000. In support of memory retention: A cooperative oral final exam. *Education* 121: 350–354.

Hinman, L. M. 2004. How to fight college cheating. *Washington Post* September 3: A19.

Huint, A. 2004. Bloom et al.'s taxonomy of the cognitive domain. *Educational Psychology Interactive* Valdosta, GA: Valdosta, State University.

Hunter, A. 2006. University marking with subtle hints of bell curve. *Archives of the New York University* September 23.

Johnson N. 2006. Test better; Teach better. *Schreyer Institute for Teaching Excellence Bulletin* (Oct. 12).

Kleinger, C. 2000. The cheating game. *US News* November 19: 22.

Korn, E. L., P. S. Albert, and L. M. McShane. 2005. Assessing surrogates as trail endpoints *Statistic in Medicine* 24 (2): 183–185.

Kruger, J., and D. Dunning. 1999. Unskilled and unaware of it: How difficulties in recognizing one's own incompetence lead to inflated self-assessment. *Journal of Personality and Social Psychology* 77 (6): 1121–1134.

Lord T. 2002. Are we cultivating "couch potatoes" in our college science lectures? In *Innovative Techniques for Large Group Instruction*, 5–8. Arlington, VA: NSTA Press.

Lord T., and S. Blaviskar. 2007. Moving students from information recitation to information understanding: Exploiting Bloom's taxonomy in creating science test questions. *Journal of College Science Teaching* 36: 40–46.

Matsuda, M. 1993. We will not be used. *Asian American Law Journal* 1: 79–84.

McChesney, K. D. 2007. What do you do when grading seems unfair? *GreatSchools: The parents' guide to school success.* Available online at *www. greatschools.net/cgi-bin/showarticle/1094.*

McDougall, A. 2005. Issues in the assessment of real-life learning. *International Federation for Information Processing* 182.

Rutherford, M. 1999. First-Term Report. *Time.* November 15.

Sleigh, M. J., and D. R. Ritzer. 2001. Encouraging student attendance. *Observer, the Journal of the American Psychological Society* 14 (9).

Strauss, E., and O. Spreen. 1998. Compendium of neuropsychological tests. 2nd ed. Oxford, UK: Oxford University Press.

Tamir, P., W. W. Welch, and J. S. Rakow. 1995. The influence of science class attitudes and teacher image on student outcomes. *Journal of Research and Development in Education* 18 (2): 26–32.

Trenholm, S. 2007. An investigation of assessment in folly asynchronous online math courses. *International Journal for Educational Integrity* 3 (2): 41–55.

Chapter 27

Varied Assessment: A Brief Introduction

William J. Straits
Department of Science Education
California State University Long Beach
Long Beach, California

R. Russell Wilke
Department of Biology
Angelo State University
San Angelo, Texas

Although often seen as a means for evaluation, assessment is first and foremost an instructional tool. As such, feedback is pivotal for instructor effectiveness as it provides a basis for correcting, developing, and refining student knowledge. The greater the depth and breadth of feedback provided, the greater its educational value. Use of multiple assessment strategies can provide students with diverse feedback, allowing students to view the subject and their understanding of it from many different perspectives. Subsequently, varied forms of assessment promote a more complete understanding of subject matter. Fortunately for the college science instructor, there are numerous strategies and techniques for providing feedback and facilitating student learning.

However, before adopting specific assessment strategies, instructors must recognize that assessments can achieve multiple purposes and must consider their reasons for assessing. Critically examining specific learning objectives throughout instruction can aide in important questions regarding assessments: To grade or not to grade? Individual or group? At the beginning, middle, or end of instruction? Of course, these are but a few of the options to consider as instructors design assessments (see Table 1 p. 148). Exploration of these considerations reveals a wealth of assessment possibilities available to college science educators.

Within the broad range of assessment possibilities, different tools can be used for given

Section 4

TABLE 1. Considerations for varied assessment, summarized from Straits and Wilke (2002)

Consideration	Description
Formal (Graded) vs. Informal (Nongraded)	Most traditional forms of assessment are formal. Formal methods are used to guide the assigning of grades. Informal methods are less intense assessments that provide immediate feedback.
Individual vs. Group Performance	Assessment is traditionally done on an individual student basis, but whole-group assessments should also be considered, particularly with inquiry learning as many inquiry activities involve cooperative learning.
Product vs. Process	Often inquiry learning lends itself to both the understanding of subject matter and the development of science process skills. The process of inquiry is extremely important and the skills developed during inquiry learning should be included in assessments.
Dynamic vs. Static	Static assessments (i.e., periodic exams covering relatively large amounts of material) are useful for establishing grades for large groups of students. However, this type of assessment focuses only on what is known at a moment and does not necessarily facilitate the learning process. Learning and assessment should be integrated and occur throughout the duration of a course.
Individual vs. Group Review	To provide greater breadth and depth of feedback to all students, lead class discussions based on completed/graded work. Solutions to the most commonly missed homework or test questions can be clarified, anonymous examples of writing assignments can be critiqued, and out-of-class reading assignments can be reviewed.

goals and objectives. Specific assessment strategies, like those developed by Angelo and Cross (1993), can be associated with various means of instruction and thus different learning outcomes. For instance, factual recall and comprehension can be assessed using objective tests, concept maps, analogy and metaphor development, essays, and paraphrasing tasks. Problem solving and application skills may be addressed with objective tests, problem sets, case studies, simulations, and prediction papers. Students' abilities to analyze and evaluate information can be informed by article critiques, design critiques, data analysis, proposal reviews, and pro/con debates.

Their abilities to use tools and processes can be developed by objective tests, problem sets, design critiques, lab and fieldwork, and simulations. Students' self-awareness can be deepened with journals, self-critiques, self-reflection papers, and project or study plans. Finally, values and attitudes may be explored using surveys, class participation, extracurricular activities related to topic, position papers, pro/con debates, and additional reading. Integrated throughout a course, the use of diverse assessment strategies allows assessment to become much more than the mere assigning of grades; with these varied strategies assessment becomes an integral part of the learning process itself.

References

Angelo, T., and K. P. Cross. 1993. *Classroom assessment techniques: A handbook for college teachers*. San Francisco, CA: Jossey-Bass.

Straits, W. J., and R. R. Wilke. 2002. Practical considerations for the development and use of assessments for inquiry-based instruction. *Journal of College Science Teaching* 31 (7): 432–435.

Chapter 28

Assessments That Assist in Motivating Students

Ellen Yerger
Department of Biology
Indiana University of Pennsylvania
Indiana, Pennsylvania

In a large lecture class of 120 freshmen for a nonscience-majors biology course, assessments are generally viewed as a problem to endure. But assessments are one of the few ways students can be reached individually. You can directly interact with each student. If used in thoughtful ways, assessments can motivate students to engage in class and to study on their own. Here are some ideas that have worked for me teaching an introductory college biology course over the past decade.

Make exams frequent, weekly or biweekly.

Frequent exams do not cover too much material and therefore students can find the time to study and are less likely to panic or give up. This counteracts the weaker planning skills of freshmen, who are not likely to start studying enough ahead of time.

Make exams short.

About 20 questions are all that are needed to cover the major topics. More questions take too much class time and overemphasize the importance of exams.

Don't take the whole class time for the exam.

Just give the exam during the first 20–30 minutes of class. As students complete the exam, let them go into the hallway to wait for the others. Once everyone is done, resume class for the remainder of the time.

Promote the class work.

Write up the exam questions directly from work you did in class. Use the exact same question that you used in class for a pair-and-share activity. This will not only motivate them to completely understand these activities the next time you do them, but it will promote class attentiveness. Don't use test bank questions unless they are right in line with what you did in class.

Reward what you want students to do.

If you want them to read the questions for self-study at the end of the textbook chapter, put some of them on the exam. If you want them to do the exercises in the study guide, put some of these on each exam. I also like to use questions from the publisher's website self-study area.

Mention once in class where you are getting some of the questions.

Students need to learn to pay attention to an employer who mentions key information once. Employees that need to be told things several times are let go in the next reorganization.

Make the test feel fair to students.

Write questions that are central to the topics you are teaching. Students will notice this and will make a renewed effort to study on the next exam. Resist making questions on tiny little details.

Actively proctor the exam.

Walk around and be visible. Watch students work and notice if they are looking sideways. Insist on nothing else on the desk, especially cell phones and backpacks. You want to be sure that no one is cheating and that all the students know that no one can cheat in your class. Students who play by the rules need to know that everyone else has to also.

Relate current topics to past topics.

It's valuable to point out to students how the current topic relates to other topics you have covered. Do this by writing a question on it. This will make them think about how it all goes together.

Line up the answer choices.

If you are asking students to choose between higher or lower levels of something, line up the different words right underneath each other so they can easily distinguish the choices.

Let the students learn from the assessment.

Once everyone has turned in their exams, pro-ject the exam onto a screen with the correct answers indicated in a bright-colored font. Don't change the visual formatting; just change the color of the answers. Resist the urge to talk. Don't go over the exam question-by-question; just show it. In my experience the students are very actively reading and talking among themselves about why certain answers are correct. Do this quickly; don't spend a lot of class time on this activity.

Send grades over a class e-mail list.

Only two columns of numbers are needed: One column is the students' ID numbers (truncated to maintain confidentiality), and the second column is the exam scores. This lets the students see their grades relative to their peers. It motivates them to see that it is possible to do better. It's nice to have a few students score 100% because the three-digit number stands out in a column of two-digit numbers. The other advantage of sending grades by e-mail is that the students' disappointment in their grades is not brought into the room when you are trying to start the next class. Also this eliminates a huge pile-up of people at the bulletin board outside the room. This helps manage the energy of the room to keep it more positive.

Assessment is more than a problem to be endured. Assessments can be structured to help you accomplish the goals of getting students engaged in class and studying on their own. It can be a positive motivator for students to focus their efforts

Index

*Page numbers in **boldface** type refer to figures or tables.*